TEST PREP SERIES

2021 Edition

VIBRANT
PUBLISHERS

GRE®

TEXT COMPLETION & SENTENCE EQUIVALENCE PRACTICE QUESTIONS
Fourth Edition

250+ solved GRE Text Completion and Sentence Equivalence questions

Answer with elaborate explanations for each question

Effective strategies and Detailed Insights to master these question types

GRE® Text Completion & Sentence Equivalence Practice Questions
Fourth Edition

Paperback ISBN-10: 1-63651-029-9
Paperback ISBN-13: 978-1-63651-029-3

E-book ISBN-10: 1-63651-030-2
E-book ISBN-13: 978-1-63651-030-9
Library of Congress Control Number: 2013909739

Vibrant Publishers books are available at special quantity discount for sales promotions, or for use in corporate training programs. For more information please write to **bulkorders@vibrantpublishers.com**

Please email feedback / corrections (technical, grammatical or spelling) to **spellerrors@vibrantpublishers.com**

To access the complete catalogue of Vibrant Publishers, visit **www.vibrantpublishers.com**

Table of Contents

This page is intentionally left blank

Dear Student,

Thank you for purchasing **GRE Text Completion and Sentence Equivalence Practice Questions.** We are committed to publishing books that are content-rich, concise and approachable enabling more students to read and make the fullest use of them. We hope this book provides the most enriching learning experience as you prepare for your **GRE** exam.

Should you have any questions or suggestions, feel free to email us at **reachus@vibrantpublishers.com**

Thanks again for your purchase. Good luck for your GRE!

- Vibrant Publishers Team

facebook.com/vibrantpublishers

///////// GRE Books in Test Prep Series //////////

6 Practice Tests for the GRE

GRE Analytical Writing: Solutions to the Real Essay Topics - Book 1

GRE Analytical Writing: Solutions to the Real Essay Topics - Book 2

GRE Analytical Writing: Solutions to the Real Essay Topics - Book 3

GRE Analytical Writing Supreme: Solutions to the Real Essay Topics

GRE Master Wordlist: 1535 Words for Verbal Mastery

GRE Quantitative Reasoning: 520 Practice Questions

GRE Reading Comprehension: Detailed Solutions to 325 Questions

GRE Words in Context: The Complete List

GRE Verbal Reasoning Supreme: Study Guide with Practice Questions

GRE Text Completion and Sentence Equivalence Practice Questions

Verbal Insights on the GRE General Test

GRE Words in Context: List 1

GRE Words in Context: List 2

GRE Words in Context: Challenging List

GRE Wordlist: 491 Essential Words

For the most updated list of books visit
www.vibrantpublishers.com

Chapter 1

Overview of the GRE General Test

The Graduate Record Examinations (GRE) General Test is required for admission to most graduate programs. The most competitive programs tend to require comparatively higher scores. This book is designed to prepare students for the GRE General Test. The GRE revised General Test was renamed in 2016 and is now known as the GRE General Test, but content and scoring of the test remain the same. Note that some graduate programs require applicants to take specialized GRE Subject Tests which will not be covered in this book. Before preparing to take the GRE, please review the admissions criteria for the programs that you are interested in applying to so that you know whether you need to take subject tests in addition to the GRE General Test. To learn more about subject tests, visit the Subject Tests section at ets.org.

The GRE General Test is not designed to measure your knowledge of specific fields. It does not measure your ability to be successful in your career or even in school. It does, however, give a reasonably accurate indication of your capabilities in certain key areas for graduate level work, such as your ability to understand complex written material, your understanding of basic mathematics, your ability to interpret data, and your capacity for reasoning and critical thinking. By using this book to prepare for the GRE General Test, you will not only improve your chances of scoring well on the test, you will also help to prepare yourself for graduate level study.

General Information of the Format of the GRE General Test

Whether you are taking the paper or computer version of the GRE General Test, the format of the test will be essentially the same. The test consists of three main components: Analytical Writing, Verbal Reasoning and Quantitative Reasoning. The total time for the test will be between 3 ½ and 3 ¾ hours, depending on the version you are taking.

The first section of the test is always the Analytical Writing component which is broken into two sections. In the first, you will be asked to write an argumentative essay that takes a position on an issue of general interest. In the second, you will be asked to analyze an argument for logical validity and soundness. You will be given 30 minutes for each section.

The remainder of the test will be split between sections devoted to Verbal Reasoning and sections devoted to Quantitative Reasoning. There will be two sections devoted to Verbal Reasoning, and another two devoted to Quantitative Reasoning. You will be given between 30-40 minutes to complete each section, and each section will contain approximately 20 questions. At any point during the test, you may be given an unscored section on either Verbal or Quantitative Reasoning; since this section will not be identified, it is important that you try your best at all times. Also, it is possible that you will be asked to complete a research section that will allow ETS to test the efficacy of new questions. If you are given a research section, it will appear at the end of your General Test. Unscored and research sections may vary in number of questions and time allotted.

Outline of the GRE General Test

The following will briefly introduce the three main components of the GRE General Test.

Analytical Writing Assessment

The first section of the GRE General Test is the Analytical Writing assessment. This component of the GRE is designed to test your ability to use basic logic and critical reasoning to make and assess arguments. The Analytical Writing assessment is broken into two assignments, each of which must be completed within 30 minutes. In the first assignment, you will be asked to develop a position on an issue of general interest. You will be given an issue and a prompt with some specific instructions on how to approach the assigned issue. You will be expected to take a position on the issue and then write a clear, persuasive and logically sound essay defending your position in correct English. You will be assessed based on your ability to effectively defend your positions with supporting evidence and valid reasoning, your skill in organizing your thoughts, and your command of English. In the second assignment, you will be presented with a passage in which the author sketches an argument for their position on an issue. Here, you will be expected to write an essay that critically evaluates their argument in terms of the evidence they use and the logical validity of their reasoning. You will be assessed based on your ability to parse the author's argument and effectively point out the strengths and weaknesses of their reasoning using good organization and correct English.

Task	Time Allowed	Answer Format
Analyze an Issue	30 minutes	Short essay on an issue of general interest that clearly and carefully addresses the prompt
Analyze an Argument	30 minutes	Short essay that analyzes another person's argument for validity, soundness and supporting evidence

The Analytical Writing assessment tests your ability to:

- Coherently develop complex ideas

- Write in a focused, organized manner

- Identify relevant evidence and use it to support your claims

- Critically evaluate another person's argument for clarity and effectiveness

- Command the elements of standard written English

Verbal Reasoning

The Verbal Reasoning portion of the GRE assesses your reading comprehension, your ability to draw inferences to fill in missing information, and your vocabulary. You will be given two sections on Verbal Reasoning, each consisting of approximately 20-25 questions and lasting 30-35 minutes. Verbal Reasoning questions on the GRE General Test are mostly multiple choice, and will be drawn from the following three types: Reading Comprehension, Text Completion, and Sentence Equivalence. Reading Comprehension questions will ask you to read a short passage several paragraphs long, and then answer questions about the passage. Text Completion questions will have a short passage with 1-3 blanks which you will need to fill in by choosing the best of several multiple choice options. The Sentence Equivalence section will ask you to fill in the blank in a passage using the two words that will complete the sentence in such a way that the meaning will be as similar as possible.

Time	Question Type	Answer Format
You will have 30-35 minutes to complete the entire section, which will include a mixture of different question types	Reading Comprehension	Multiple choice: select one answer choice Multiple choice: select one or more answer choices Highlight a section of text
	Text Completion	Multiple choice: fill in one or more blanks to complete the text
	Sentence Equivalence	Multiple choice: select the two options that produce two sentences with the most similar meanings

The Verbal Reasoning section tests your ability to:

- Comprehend, interpret and analyze complex passages in standard written English

- Apply sophisticated vocabulary in context

- Draw inferences about meaning and authorial intent based on written material

Quantitative Reasoning

The Quantitative Reasoning section of the GRE evaluates your ability to use basic mathematics, read and interpret graphs and figures and engage in basic reasoning involving math and numbers. You will be given two sections on Quantitative Reasoning, each with about 20-25 questions. You will have 35-40 minutes to complete each section. There are two basic question types, multiple choice and numerical entry. For multiple choice questions, you will be asked to choose the best answer or answers from several possibilities; for numerical entry questions, you will be asked to enter a numerical answer from your own calculations. Some questions will be designed to test your knowledge of basic algebra and geometry; others will be designed to test your ability to read and interpret different presentations of data.

Time	Question Type	Answer Format
You will have 35-40 minutes to complete the entire section, which will include a mixture of different question types	Multiple Choice	• Select one answer choice • Select one or more answer choices
	Numeric Entry	• Solve the problem through calculation and enter a numeric value
	Quantitative Comparison	Evaluate two quantities to decide whether one is greater than the other, whether they are equal, or whether a relationship cannot be determined
	Data Interpretation	• Multiple choice: choose the best answer or answers • Numeric entry: enter a value

The Quantitative Reasoning section tests your ability to:

- Use mathematical tools such as basic arithmetic, geometry, algebra and statistics

- Understand, interpret and analyze quantitative information

- Apply basic mathematical and data interpretation skills to real-world information and problems

Paper Based and Computer Based GRE General Test

The Paper Based GRE General Test

If you are taking the paper-based version of the test, the format will be slightly different than the computer-based version. The typical format for the paper version of the test will be as follows:

Component	Number of Questions	Time Allowed
Analytical Writing	1 Analyze an Issue 1 Analyze an Argument	30 minutes 30 minutes
Verbal Reasoning (2 sections)	25 questions per section	35 minutes per section
Quantitative Reasoning (2 sections)	25 questions per section	40 minutes per section

Note that if you are taking the paper based test, you will not be given an unscored section or a research section. You will enter all answers in your test booklet, and you will be provided with an ETS calculator for doing computations. You will not be allowed to use your own calculator.

The Computer Based GRE General Test

If you are taking the computer-based version of the test, the format will be slightly different than the paper-based version. Also, unlike the paper-based test, the Verbal Reasoning and Quantitative Reasoning sections of the computer based version is partially adaptive. This means that the computer will adapt the test to your performance. Since there are two sections each of Verbal Reasoning and Quantitative Reasoning, the difficulty of the second section will depend on how well you did on the first section. The format for the computer-based version of the test will be as follows:

Component	Number of Questions	Time Allowed
Analytical Writing	1 Analyze an Issue 1 Analyze an Argument	30 minutes 30 minutes
Verbal Reasoning (2 sections)	Approximately 20 questions per section	30 minutes per section
Quantitative Reasoning (2 sections)	Approximately 20 questions per section	35 minutes per section
Unscored	Variable	Variable
Research	Variable	Variable

While taking the computer based GRE General Test:

- You can review and preview questions within a section, allowing you to budget your time to deal with the questions that you find most difficult.

- You will be able to mark questions within a section and return to them later. This means that if you find a question especially difficult, you will be able to move on to other questions and return to the one that you had trouble with, provided that you stay within the time limit for the section.

- You will be able to change or edit your answers within a section. This means that if you realize that you made a mistake, you can go back and correct yourself provided you stay within the time limit for the section.

- You will have an onscreen calculator during the Quantitative Reasoning portions of the test, allowing you to quickly complete any necessary computations.

Registering for the GRE

Before you register to take the GRE, be sure to consider your schedule and any special accommodations that you may need. Be aware that the availability of testing dates may vary according to your location, and that paper based testing only takes place on certain set dates. Be sure to give yourself plenty of time to prepare for the GRE, and be sure that you know the deadlines for score reporting and application deadlines for all the schools you are applying to. For general information about deadlines and the GRE, visit GRE section at ets.org. For more information on how to register for the GRE, visit the Register for GRE section at ets.org. For information on special accommodations for disabled students, visit Disabilities section at ets.org.

How the GRE General Test is Scored

Scoring for the Analytical Writing Section

In the Analytical Writing section, you will be scored on a scale of 0-6 in increments of .5. The Analytical Writing measure emphasizes your ability to engage in reasoning and critical thinking over your facility with the finer points of grammar. The highest scores of 5.5-6.0 are given to work that is generally superior in every respect - sustained analysis of complex issues, coherent argumentation and excellent command of English language. The lowest scores of 0.0-0.5 are given to work that is completely off topic or so poorly composed as to be incoherent.

Scoring for the Verbal and Quantitative Reasoning Sections

The Verbal and Quantitative Reasoning sections are now scored on a scale of 130-170 in 1 point increments.

General Strategies for Taking the GRE

There are strategies you can apply that will greatly increase your odds of performing well on the GRE. The following is a list of strategies that will help to improve your chances of performing well on the GRE:

- Review basic concepts in math, logic and writing.

- Work through the test-taking strategies offered in this book.

- Work through mock GRE tests until you feel thoroughly comfortable with the types of questions you will see.

- As you are studying for the GRE, focus your energy on the types of questions that give you the most difficulty.

- Learn to guess wisely. For many of the questions on the Verbal and Quantitative Reasoning Sections, the correct answer is in front of you - you only need to correctly identify it. Especially for questions that you find difficult, you should hone your ability to dismiss the options that are clearly wrong and make an educated guess about which one is right.

- Answer every question. You won't lose any points for choosing the wrong answer, so even a wild guess that might or might not be right is better than no answer at all.

Preparing for Test Day and Taking the GRE

How you prepare for the test is completely up to you, and will depend on your own test-taking preferences and the amount of time you can devote to studying for the test. At the very least, before you take the test, you should know the basics of what is covered on the test along with the general guidelines for taking the GRE. This book is designed to provide you with the basic information you need, and give you the opportunity to prepare thoroughly for the GRE General Test.

Although there is no set way to prepare for the GRE, as a general rule you will want to

- Learn the basics about the test - what is being tested, the format, and how the test is administered.

- Familiarize yourself with the specific types of questions that you will see on the GRE General Test.

- Review skills such as basic math, reading comprehension, and writing.

- Learn about test-taking strategies.

- Take a mock GRE test to practice applying your test-taking skills to an actual test.

Remember, you don't need to spend an equal amount of time on each of these areas to do well on the GRE - allot your study time to your own needs and preferences. The following are some suggestions to help you make the final preparations for your test, and help you through the test itself:

Preparing for Test Day

- In the time leading up to your test, practice, then practice some more. Practice until you are confident with the material.

- Know when your test is, and when you need to be at the testing center.

- Make a "practice run" to your testing center, so that you can anticipate how much time you will need to allow to get there.

- Understand the timing and guidelines for the test and plan accordingly. Remember that you are not allowed to eat or drink while taking the GRE, although you will be allowed to snack or drink during some of the short breaks during testing. Plan accordingly.

- Know exactly what documentation you will need to bring with you to the testing center.

- Relax, especially in the day or night before your test. If you have studied and practiced wisely, you will be well prepared for the test. You may want to briefly glance over some test preparation materials, but cramming the night before will not be productive.

- Eat well and get a good night's sleep. You will want to be well rested for the test.

The Test Day

- Wake up early to give yourself plenty of time to eat a healthy breakfast, gather the necessary documentation, pack a snack and a water bottle, and make it to the testing center well before your test is scheduled to start.

- Have confidence: You've prepared well for the test, and there won't be any big surprises. You may not know the answers to some questions, but the format will be exactly like what you've been practicing.

- While you are taking the test, don't panic. The test is timed, and students often worry that they will run out of time and miss too many questions. The sections of the test are designed so that many students will not finish them, so don't worry if you don't think you can finish a section on time. Just try to answer as many questions as you can, as accurately as possible.

- Remember the strategies and techniques that you learn from this book, and apply them wherever possible.

Frequently Asked Questions

General Questions

What changes have been made to the GRE revised General Test?

The GRE revised General Test (introduced on August 1, 2011) is now known as the GRE General Test. Only the name of the test has changed. Content and scoring have remained the same. Study materials that reference the GRE revised General Test are still valid and may be used for test preparation.

Why did the name of the test change from GRE revised General Test to GRE General Test?

The name of the test was changed from GRE revised General Test to GRE General Test in 2016 because the word "revised" was no longer needed to distinguish the version of the GRE prior to August 1, 2011. The scores from that version of the test are no longer reported.

How do I get ready to take GRE General Test?

To take the GRE General Test, there are several steps you'll need to take:

- Find out what prospective graduate/professional programs require: Does the program you're interested in require additional testing beyond the GRE General Test? What is the deadline for receipt of scores?

- Sign up for a test date. You need to sign up for any GRE testing. For computer based testing, there will generally be numerous dates to choose from, although acting in a timely manner is essential so that you have plenty of time to prepare and are guaranteed that your scores will be sent and received on time. For paper based testing, testing dates are much more restricted, so if you know that you will need to take the paper based GRE General Test, make arrangements well in advance of the application deadline for your program.

- Use this book and the resources provided by ETS to familiarize yourself with both the format of the GRE and the types of questions you will face. Even if you are confident about taking the test, it is essential to prepare for the test.

Does the GRE General Test Measure my proficiency in specific subject areas?

No. The GRE General Test is designed to measure general proficiency in reading, critical reasoning, and working with data, all abilities that are critical to graduate work. However, you won't be tested on your knowledge of any specific field.

Where can I get additional information on the GRE General Test?

Educational Testing Service (ETS), the organization that administers the GRE, has an informative website entirely devoted to information about the test at the GRE section at ets.org. There, you can find links that further explain how to sign up for testing, fees, score reporting and much more.

Preparing for the Test

How should I start to prepare for the test?

The first thing you should do is thoroughly familiarize yourself with the format of the GRE General Test. Once you've decided whether you're taking the paper based test, or the computerized version, learn exactly what you can expect from the version of the test you're taking - how many sections there are, how many questions per section, etc. You can find general information about the structure of the test earlier in this chapter.

How do I prepare for the questions I will be asked on the GRE General Test?

There are plenty of resources by Vibrant Publishers, including this book to help you prepare for the questions you will face on the GRE General Test. A list of books is provided at the end of this book. For the most updated list, you may visit www.vibrantpublishers.com.

How much should I study/practice for the GRE?

Study and practice until you feel comfortable with the test. Practice, practice and practice some more until you feel confident about test day!

Are there additional materials I can use to get even more practice?

Yes. ETS offers a free full-length practice test that can be downloaded from the GRE section at ets.org. Also, after you have signed up for testing through ETS, you are eligible for some further test preparation materials free of additional charge.

Test Content

How long the GRE General Test is?

- The computer based version of the test is around 3 hours and 45 minutes including short breaks.

- The paper based version of the test will take around 3 hours and 30 minutes.

What skills does the GRE test?

In general, the GRE is designed to test your proficiency in certain key skills that you will need for graduate level study. More specifically:

- **The Analytical Writing section** tests your ability to write about complex ideas in a coherent, focused fashion as well as your ability to command the conventions of standard written English, provide and evaluate relevant evidence, and critique other points of view.

- **The Verbal Reasoning section** tests your ability to understand, interpret and analyze complex passages, use reasoning to draw inferences about written material, and use sophisticated vocabulary in context.

- **The Quantitative Reasoning section** tests your knowledge of basic, high school-level mathematics, as well as your ability to analyze and interpret data.

What level of math is required for the Quantitative Reasoning section?

You will be expected to know high school level math - arithmetic, and basic concepts in algebra and geometry. You will also be expected to be able to analyze and interpret data presented in tables and graphs.

Scoring and Score Reporting

How are the sections of the GRE General Test scored?

The GRE General Test is scored as follows:

- **The Verbal Reasoning section** is scored in 1-point increments on a scale of 130-170.

- **The Quantitative Reasoning section** is scored in 1-point increments on a scale of 130-170.

- **The Analytical Writing section** is scored on a scale of 0-6 in increments of .5.

When will my score be reported?

It depends on which version of the test you are taking, and also when you decide to take the GRE General Test. In general, scores for the computer based version of the test are reported within two weeks; for the paper based test, they are reported within six weeks. Check the GRE section at ets.org for updates on score reporting and deadlines.

How long will my scores be valid?

In general, your score for the GRE General Test will remain valid for five years. The following are some specifications about score validity:

For those who have yet to take the test, or have taken it on or after July 1, 2016, scores are valid for five years after the test administration date.

- For those who have taken the test between August 1, 2011 and June 30, 2016, scores are valid for five years after the testing year. For example, scores from a test taken in April 2015 would be valid until June 2020.

- Scores from August 2011 are valid until June 30, 2017.

Other Questions

Do business schools accept the GRE instead of the GMAT?

An increasing number of business schools accept the GRE as a substitute for the more standard test for admission to an MBA program, the GMAT. Before you decide to take the GRE instead of the GMAT, make sure that the programs you are interested in applying to will accept the GRE. You can find a list of business schools that currently accept the GRE in the GRE section at ets.org.

How is the GRE administered?

The GRE is administered at designated testing centers, where you can take the test free from distraction in a secure environment that discourages cheating. The computer based version of the test is administered continuously year round at designated testing centers. In areas where computer based testing is unavailable, the paper based version of the test is administered at most three times a year on designated dates. For information on testing centers in your area and important dates, visit the GRE section at ets.org.

I have a disability that requires me to ask for special accommodation while taking the test - what sort of accommodations are offered?

ETS does accommodate test-takers with disabilities. For information on procedures, visit the GRE section at ets.org.

Will there be breaks during testing?

Yes. You will have a 10 minute break during the test. On the computer based version of the test, the 10 minute break will fall after you have completed the first three sections of the test. On the paper based version, you will be given a 10 minute break following the Analytical Writing sections.

Will I be given scratch paper?

If you are taking the computer based version of the test, you will be given as much scratch paper as you need. If you are taking the paper based version of the test, you won't be allowed to use scratch paper, however, you will be allowed to write in your test booklet.

Should I bring a calculator to the test?

No. If you are taking the computer based version of the test, there will be an onscreen calculator for you to use. If you are taking the paper based version of the test, an ETS-approved calculator will be issued to you at the testing center.

Chapter **2**

Introduction to Text Completion

Text Completion questions are designed to further test your ability to understand what you read. They will also test your vocabulary, particularly your ability to apply sophisticated vocabulary in context. You will be asked to read a short passage of 1-5 sentences. There will be 1-3 blanks in the passage where a crucial word is missing. You will need to fill in each blank using several options provided.

The passages used for Text Completion questions will be drawn from a variety of topics, including the physical, biological and social sciences, the arts and the humanities, business and everyday life. As with Reading Comprehension questions you do not need to be an expert on the topic covered, you only need to read the passage attentively enough to be able to pick the right word for the blank.

All Text Completion questions will be in a multiple choice format. Each passage will have 1-3 blanks, and you will be given several options to choose from to fill in the blanks. Generally, passages with only one blank will have five options to choose from, while those with 2-3 blanks will have only three options per blank.

What does a Text Completion question look like?

Text Completion questions will always be based off a short passage of one or more sentences. The passage will have 1-3 blanks. You will be asked to read the passage and get a feel of what words will best complete it using several options given. Below are examples of what Text Completion questions will look like on the GRE General Test:

For each blank select one entry from the corresponding column of choices. Fill all blanks in the way that best completes the text.

1. The later Roman Empire was continually (i) _____ invasions of nomadic and semi-nomadic peoples who were often themselves (ii) _____ by marauding tribes from the Central Asian steppes.

<table>
<tr><td align="center">Blank (i)</td><td align="center">Blank (ii)</td></tr>
</table>

Blank (i)
delighted
threatened
enthralled

Blank (ii)
displaced
dismissed
averred

2. Harry's _____ performance on the project both failed to impress his superiors and helped to lose the company an important client.

rapacious
desultory
indomitable
arcane
indefatigable

Answer Key

The correct answers are:

1. (i) threatened   (ii) displaced

2. desultory

What skills do Text Completion questions test?

Text Completion questions test your ability to understand complex sentences and passages. They also test your ability to use sophisticated vocabulary in context and your ability to use reasoning to complete an idea based on incomplete information. Some key skills that are tested include your ability to

- understand a text holistically and be able to determine the meaning of individual components

- use reasoning to fill in important gaps in information

- understand high level vocabulary

- apply vocabulary in context

Key facts about Text Completion questions

- Questions will be based off short passages 1-5 sentences long

- For each passage, you will need to fill in 1-3 blanks using 3-5 options provided

- Passages will be on a variety of topics including the physical, biological and social sciences, the arts and the humanities, business and everyday life

- Questions will be answerable based on the information in the passage alone and your ability to apply vocabulary

Strategies for Text Completion Questions

Depending on what version of the GRE you are taking, you will have 30 or 35 minutes to complete each Verbal Reasoning section. While budgeting your time is important, Text Completion questions are different than Reading Comprehension questions and require you to alter your strategies accordingly. In the first place, the passages used for Text Completion questions will generally be much shorter than those used for Reading Comprehension questions. This means that it will take you less time to carefully read a passage for a Text Completion question than it would for you to carefully read a Reading Comprehension passage. Moreover, Text Completion questions are much more focused, and to answer them effectively, you may need to grasp subtle aspects of sentence structure. While you will not want to get hung up on a single Text Completion question, you will generally want to read the passages with more care than those used for Reading Comprehension questions. Do not try to skim through Text Completion questions. If you feel that you are taking too much time on a single question, either make an educated guess or bookmark it in case you have time later and then move on.

As with Reading Comprehension, do not let the subject matter of the passage throw you off - your ability to correctly answer these questions will not rely on your expertise in any particular area. When answering Text Completion questions, one of the key skills you will need is the ability to grasp the overall meaning of the passage even with certain words missing. You will then need to apply your understanding of the passage, coupled with your grasp of key transitional words in the passage, to correctly choose the word that best fits with the overall meaning of the passage. Where Reading Comprehension questions test your ability to grasp general meanings, Text Completion tests your ability to read carefully and understand more subtle cues about the meaning of specific sections of text.

The key skills for Text Completion are reading closely and applying vocabulary in context. You'll need to get a quick idea of what the passage is about, and the general tone, but beyond that, you need to be able to see how specific words fit into the whole passage. Focus most of your attention on the individual meanings of different components of the passage. Often there are overt indications of which words will best complete the passage; either the word you need to complete the passage will be essentially defined in another clause, or the context will strongly suggest that you use a word with the opposite meaning to what has already been said. These contextual indicators are quite valuable, so keep a close eye out for them. Also, because vocabulary is a more important part of Text Completion questions, anything you can do to review or improve your vocabulary will probably be helpful.

- Read the passage carefully - do not skim

- Focus on significant words to help you grasp precise meanings

- Keep an eye out for sections of the passage that either closely match or negate the definition of one of the word options

- Apply vocabulary in context

What follows are some more specific strategies for answering Text Completion questions. In the next chapter, you'll have a chance to put your skills to the test through several practice questions and learn how to hone them in the answers and explanations that follow.

Review Vocabulary

Anything that you can do to strengthen your vocabulary prior to the test will be helpful. Although the GRE General Test does not feature any section that is strictly designed to test vocabulary, the Verbal Reasoning section assumes a fairly high level vocabulary. Your command of sophisticated vocabulary is especially important for the Text Completion and Sentence Equivalence sections, since you will need to identify the right word to fill in a blank. If you are not confident of your vocabulary, do what you can to improve it as preparation for the test (this will serve you well in graduate school as well). Note that in many cases you will not need to know a precise definition of a word, but you do need to have a general sense of what it means. There are several things you can do to improve your vocabulary for the test:

- Review lists of common "GRE words" such as the one included in this book

- Use a vocabulary builder

- Get a sense of key Greek or Latin root words and what they mean - many words in English are based on Greek or Latin words, and knowing the meaning of a few key Greek or Latin words can help you figure out the meanings of numerous English words

Get a General Feel of the Passage

Before you try to fill in any blanks, get a general sense of what the passage says, and the tone. Doing this will help you get a general feel whether a particular word fits or not. As you read the passage, pay close attention to words that may signal a shift in tone or perspective. Such words give insight into the meaning of the passage as a whole, and can also tell you something about the particular phrase that you'll need to complete.

Pay Special Attention to Significant Words

Certain key words can give tremendous insight into the meaning of a passage or phrase. Many times your ability to correctly answer Text Completion questions will hinge on whether you are able to detect qualifying words in a passage. Be especially alert for words like "although" and "despite", which suggests that the what has been said so far is about to be qualified. Also keep an eye out for words like "therefore", "moreover" and "thus" which suggest summation or additional support for points that have already been made.

Don't Assume That You Should Always Fill In the First Blank First

Sometimes the order in which you fill in the blanks won't matter. For some questions, however, it will be difficult to fill in one blank without first correctly filling in another blank. The first blank won't always be the one you should try to fill in first - sometimes you will need to reason backwards through the passage. Keep in mind that some Text Completion questions are very straightforward - others are designed to test your reasoning, so be prepared to use more than just vocabulary to find the correct answer.

Come up With Your Own Words to Fill in the Blanks

As you read through the passage, try to think of words that would fill in the blanks; then, compare the answer options given to the words you have thought of and try to select similar words from among the options. If you are unsure of what some of the words mean and cannot identify similar words, try to eliminate words with opposite meanings to the words you picked.

Check Your Work

Always re-read the passage with the answer(s) you have selected and filled in to see whether the passage is grammatical and makes sense with the options you have chosen. Even if your choice seemed right, if it does not produce a coherent, grammatically correct passage, it isn't the correct answer.

Use Process of Elimination

You can apply process of elimination to Text Completion questions as well. Sometimes, you may quickly identify the correct answer or answers, but other times you may be uncertain. In cases where you don't find the right answer to be immediately obvious, use process of elimination to narrow the options. Many times a word with the opposite meaning from the correct answer will appear among the choices - you can immediately dismiss such words. Other times you will find words that simply have nothing to do with the context, and these can be dismissed as well. As with any other multiple choice question, eliminating obviously wrong answers will always increase your odds of getting the right answer.

This page is intentionally left blank

Chapter 3

Practice Questions for Text Completion

1. Although he took great pains as an educator to (i) _____ a love of reasoning and virtue in his students, Athenian (ii) _____ of the day considered Socrates to be a/an (iii) _____, intent on destroying their authority and subverting the youth of Athens.

Blank (i)	Blank (ii)	Blank (iii)
ingurgitate	portents	centurion
importune	potentates	iconoclast
inculcate	profligates	neophyte

2. Stephens professes to have no bias, but a discerning analysis of his article "Our Youth Must Work" reveals that the author employs (i) _____ to create an ingenious yet invalid argument aimed at misleading readers into agreeing with a youth service program that penalizes students from the lower socio-economic echelons in favor of their (ii) _____ peers who will simply be able to buy their way out of the proposed two years of community or military service.

Blank (i)	Blank (ii)
dissimulation	erudite
hubris	ostentatious
sophistry	patrician

3. Because of crime distribution data, criminologists can add to their qualitative analysis a quantitative dynamic; this _____ of approaches allows for greater insight.

confluence
reduction
petulance
reluctance
diaspora

4. While the original conception of rhetoric confined its uses to political discourse, many people now agree that the art of debate _____ every field of study.

permits
permeates
aggrandizes
aggravates
rectifies

5. The crude tools of human civilizations leave a trail throughout time that _____ even when the written records of events become unclear or seem to be in direct contradiction to one another.

discontinue
perdures
excavates
derides
beguiles

6. The various psychosocial variables that constitute the human mind cannot be understood through strict experimentation without also considering the _____ such experiments inherently introduce in the subject.

prejudices
pellucidity
impartiality
riposte
plutocracy

7.   Competition is highly desirable in a free market economy – the concentration of market capital in relatively few enterprises can _____ economic health by forcing customers to pay prices they can barely afford.

attenuate
consecrate
commiserate
alleviate
fulminate

8.   Looking back, he was amazed by his own (i) _____. His experienced friends told him that there was no fast way to learn guitar. They said that he would just have to accept a slow progression of skill. But he (ii) _____ this advice every step of the way, pushing his hands as hard as he could. Now that he was staring down the harsh reality of carpal tunnel syndrome, he wished that he had taken their advice.

Blank (i)	Blank (ii)
pensiveness	articulated
reticence	flouted
obstinacy	expounded

9.   Gary always resented the way people (i) _____ television. If he ever mentioned a program he had recently watched he was always met with reprimands from others. They told him how television was a waste, how it rotted his brain. The (ii) _____ was staggering: Gary knew that these same people also watched television; they just denied it in public in order to put on airs. And what was so sacrosanct about the other forms of media? There were trashy novels, just like there were trashy television programs.

Blank (i)	Blank (ii)
derided	equanimity
bolstered	duplicity
protracted	sublimity

10.   He had never ridden a motorcycle before but the notion (i) _____ him. The idea of cruising across the country instilled him with a feeling a freedom he had never experienced before. He had always been (ii) _____, preferring the safety of an office environment to anything else.

Blank (i)
vetoed
exhilarated
censured

Blank (ii)
obdurate
milquetoast
contrarian

11.   The newfound money couldn't (i) _____ the sorrow. Tiffany had inherited more money than she would ever be able to spend, but she would rather have had her parents back. She couldn't help but (ii) _____ the comments that her friends made about her situation. They reprimanded her for her sullenness, told her that she was lucky to be in the situation that she was.

Blank (i)
masticate
interpolate
alleviate

Blank (ii)
lionize
oblige
begrudge

12.   Howard knew that the story of the musician who trades integrity for money was (i) _____, but it felt new to him. He was being offered the chance to sign a recording contract, but a quick glance at the fine print told him that he would be signing away his dignity. The contract would guarantee him fame and fortune, but it would license his music to the highest bidder and charge (ii) _____ prices to his loyal fans.

Blank (i)
cliche
facetious
metaphorical

Blank (ii)
inconsequential
judicious
appalling

13.   Horoscopes are somewhat like fortune cookie fortunes - they sound true, because they are based on human nature and human behavior, both of which are homogenous and therefore fairly predictable. Furthermore, horoscopes are highly generic or shrouded in metaphor whose (i) _____ can easily be changed to meet the (ii) _____ of our lives and can be applied to almost everyone almost anytime.

Blank (i)
palpability
elucidation
omnipotence

Blank (ii)
exigencies
generalizations
generalities

14.   The flu of 1918 infected an estimated 500 million people worldwide, killing 3 to 5 percent of the world's population within two years. Although the (i) _____ was entirely unpreventable and particularly deadly, it galvanized leaders world-wide to develop a (ii) _____ strategy for dealing with mass infections, leading ultimately, to the creation of the World Health Organization.

Blank (i)
endemic
pandemic
epidemic

Blank (ii)
congruous
germane
refractory

15.   The combined _____ of scientists present at the time of the launch could not have enabled them to predict the unanticipated events predicated by what should have been a routine display of military prowess.

demeanor
heresy
efficacy
acumen
callosity

16.   At a loss to explain the overwhelming popularity of today's insipid TV reality shows, critics have come
       to the conclusion that viewers who are obsessed with reality programs are drawn to the _____
       lifestyles depicted and allow the radiance of the stars' lives override the spurious dilemmas and
       dubious coping skills of the so-called stars.

refulgent
austere
laudable
monotonous
sanctimonious

17.   The more loudly and adamantly he denied any involvement with the crime, the less the jury believed
       him. Clearly his _____ would not pass muster with them, and he had no doubt their deliberations
       would be short and to the point: guilty!

dyspepsia
harangue
approbation
peregrination
gaucherie

18.   Strict laws prohibiting dog fighting aim to reduce the number of dogs injured or killed each year in this
       heinous but lucrative industry by targeting those truly responsible, not the dogs who are bred and
       forced to fight, but the depraved owners who perpetuate this _____ of sport for personal glory and
       financial gain.

tirade
artifice
debauch
travesty
apparition

19.   Perhaps the most _____ of any play ever performed, James Carthwaite's rendition of "Born to be Wilde," based on the art and antics of the late Oscar Wilde, took eight hours to perform and was executed over two consecutive nights - or would have been had it not closed down halfway through the first night.

pedantic
odious
onerous
moribund
prolix

20.   A few of us watched in awe from the (i) _____ above town as the last of our makeshift barriers (ii) _____ and Cowtown, built on the shifting alluvial soils of the Temash Delta, crumbled and was swept away like so much (iii) _____ being sucked down a drain.

Blank (i)	Blank (ii)	Blank (iii)
estuary	capitulated	calumny
ravine	countenanced	aspersion
butte	assuaged	detritus

21.   More people living longer lives due to worldwide improvements in health care and nutrition translates to the need for nursing homes across the country to develop their _____ care capacity to attend to the needs of an aging population over the long run.

ameliorative
palliative
regressive
salubrious
proprietary

22. Henry VIII may have been the most powerful man in the world in his time, but as a monarch he certainly was not fortuitous when it came to producing a male heir to ascend to the throne. His _____ included Prince Edward who died in childhood and the Princesses, Mary and Elizabeth.

progenitors
scions
devisees
lineage
promulgations

23. Though its name would suggest it is (i) _____, the Kiss-Kiss, a leech with a predilection for human blood, (ii)_____ infiltrates homes and ensconce themselves among the bedding to ambush its prey - us! Once thought to be rare, recent Kiss-Kiss inventories confirm of the kiss-kiss bug, a vector of Chagras Disease, is (iii) _____ in the southwestern US, Mexico, and most parts of Central-America.

Blank (i)	Blank (ii)	Blank (iii)
innocuous	surreptitiously	ubiquitous
portentous	precipitously	exiguous
accumbent	quintessentially	anomalous

24. _____, once thought to be the result of poor motivation or bad genetics and the fault of the released prisoners rather than the institutions that released them, has institutional and social dimensions that are far beyond the control of the ex-offender, and, that unabated, virtually enslave ex-offenders to criminal lifestyles ensuring that they become permanent residents of our penal institutions.

Gasconade
Recidivism
Exfiltration
Chicanery
Attenuation

25. In the story the "Confessions of Felix Krull, Confidence Man," the young protagonist, Felix feigns a serious illness to (i) _____ both his mother and the family physician who is also her lover, that he is indeed very sick. Felix describes the almost intolerable pleasure that his performance brings him, saying, "I was beyond beatific, absolutely (ii) _____ with the alternate tension and relaxation necessary to give reality, in my own eyes and others, to a condition that did not exist."

Blank (i)
suborn
cajole
inveigh

Blank (ii)
desultory
rapturous
aberrant

26. In light of his many (i) _____ with the ladies and his illicit dealings in pornography, the pastor's comments on the on the aberrations of deviate behavior among parishioners was viewed as sanctimonious (ii) _____ and readily dismissed.

Blank (i)
adumbrations
dilettantes
peccadilloes

Blank (ii)
chit-chat
invective
cant

27. Although the problems identified with the SR7 (i) _____ Rover, designed to collect data and soil samples from the surface of Mars have been publicized extensively over the past few weeks, they are not of much consequence when considered individually. However, the cumulative effect of the myriad of (ii) _____ must be factored into scientists' decision to launch the Rover or (iii) _____.

Blank (i)	Blank (ii)	Blank (iii)
Canard	gimmicks	take the bull by the horns
Reconnaissance	gimcracks	throw the baby out with the bath water
Alliance	glitches	go back to the drawing board

28. Although Aristotle did not have a high opinion of octopi, calling them "stupid creatures," their reputation as problem solvers and critical thinkers has recently been _____, largely due to the antics of a Delhi zoo octopus named Andy who selects what he wants to eat from a menu of 28 fresh fish choices, regularly ambushes his fellow tank mates just for fun, and has to be kept in a specialized tank because he has learned to pick all traditional tank locks.

ruminated
bifurcated
expedited
ameliorated
scintillated

29. Growing a vegetable garden may seem difficult, but anyone can do it. Home-grown (i) _____ is tastier, healthier, and cheaper than what you find in grocery stores. It is important to plan out your (ii) _____ – research what plants grow best in your region, find out how much sun the plants require, and make sure you have the tools you need. After planting your vegetables, tend them daily. Watering and weeding are a must. Once your (iii) _____ is ripe, harvest and enjoy the fruits of your labor!

Blank (i)	Blank (ii)	Blank (iii)
calumny	acreage	concurrence
produce	nadir	fruitage
morasses	quagmire	exculpation

30. (i) _____ criminals are an increasing threat to both private companies and the world economic system. Not only were five computer programmers recently arrested for hacking into the servers of several American companies and stealing 160,000,000 credit card numbers, but their leader was also caught hacking into the Nasdaq stock exchange. The America's stock exchange is far from alone in its (ii) _____. 53 percent of the world's exchanges have fallen victim to the (iii) _____ of hackers in the last year.

Blank (i)	Blank (ii)	Blank (iii)
Cyber	aversion	puissance
Cryptic	perfidy	nostrum
Captious	vulnerability	cynosure

31. General Motors saw a 19 percent fall in net income due to a (i) _____ drop in profits in Asia. Recently poor economic conditions have made Europe the largest trouble spot for the company, but GM narrowed losses in Europe while registering higher than normal losses in Asia. A rise in (ii) _____ from the Japanese, Korean, and Australian automobile markets contributed to losses in the region. Despite a 4 percent gain in North America, GM is in trouble if it does not come up with strategies to perform more (iii) _____.

Blank (i)	Blank (ii)	Blank (iii)
propitious	competitors	erratically
precipitous	assailant	consistently
promontory	hindrances	pedantically

32. To combat the fears of Russification, Christianization, and general assimilation, Tatar reformers had to (i) _____ the importance of strengthening Tatar cultural identity. This, along with a more flexible (and therefore in many ways more durable) (ii) _____ of Islam, helped the Tatar community retain their ethnic identity while developing a modernized secular relationship with Russia. To this end, writers like Amirkhan highlighted the capability of Tatars to embrace reforms and secular education while still (iii) _____ their Tatar identity.

Blank (i)	Blank (ii)	Blank (iii)
desiccate	aesthetic	abdicating
accentuate	indoctrination	perpetuating
abrogate	apperception	gainsaying

33. Proposed solutions to the conflict take the form of the packaged and phased approaches – addressing all the (i) _____ of the conflict in one fell swoop versus creating a schedule to deal with each question one at a time. The first allows for resolution in a single document and enables everyone to focus immediately on (ii) _____ action. Unfortunately, it is less politically viable and less flexible. The second (iii) _____ immediate pressures making leadership able to engage in substantive conversation, but risks derailing due to changes in external circumstance and inertia.

Blank (i)	Blank (ii)	Blank (iii)
inaccuracies	tangible	alleviates
perquisites	ephemeral	exterminating
components	amorphous	implicates

34. The Abkhazian uprisings against the Russian Empire were unsuccessful, but had a lasting impact on the (i) _____ of the region. Some Abkhaz fled of their own accord – mostly those who were (ii) _____ to the anti-Russian revolts. Others left involuntarily, as victims of the ethnic cleansings in the North Caucasus. During the late 1800s the Russian Army forced the Abkhaz, Adyghe, Ubykh, and Abaza peoples from their homelands. The majority of these (iii) _____ populations settled in the Ottoman Empire.

Blank (i)	Blank (ii)	Blank (iii)
demographics	copasetic	complacent
recidivism	sympathetic	appeased
raiment	phlegmatic	dispossessed

35. Wildflowers are faithful to their bumblebee "sweethearts." In a recent study, (i) _____ found that wildflowers produce fewer seeds when a single bumblebee species is removed. Apparently, the plant/pollinator relationship is (ii) _____. Each bee species focuses on a single plant variety until it finishes blooming, thus increasing the fidelity of the species. The result is a rise in seed production. The study underlined the importance of (iii) _____ in the conservation of ecosystems as the removal of a bee species resulted in decreased plant reproduction.

Blank (i)	Blank (ii)	Blank (iii)
Cryptologists	monogamous	anathemas
Geologists	polygamous	surfeit
Ecologists	hypergamous	biodiversity

36. Researchers have discovered (i) _____ method for targeting and manipulating any gene in the human genome. An RNA-guided enzyme found in the Streptococcus bacteria could (ii) _____ be used to cure many genetic diseases as well as to reprogram stem and adult cells. The (iii) _____ of this discovery are far-reaching, but scientists are not yet sure what all the possibilities are. Using the RNA-guided enzyme is relatively simple, which makes the scientific community hopeful in regards to its real world applications.

Blank (i)	Blank (ii)	Blank (iii)
a superfluous	abstractly	impositions
an expedient	presumptively	implications
an imprudent	dubiously	inhibitions

37.   Scientists have long been fascinated by superfluids, such as liquid helium, since they seem to defy the laws of (i) _____. Moving without the (ii) _____ of gravity or surface tension, superfluids have zero viscosity and can squeeze through holes the size of a molecule or climb up the side of a glass. They have been (iii) _____ to remain in motion for years after the centrifuge containing them has stopped spinning.

Blank (i)	Blank (ii)	Blank (iii)
geology	opprobrium	observed
physics	celerity	obliterated
biology	interference	envisioned

38.   A series of intense storms and rising water levels over the last several years has resulted in (i) _____ in erosion on beaches across the country. As a result, many states are considering beach nourishment projects: replacing the large amounts of lost sediment with similar material either transported from other locations or manufactured. This new sand is usually (ii) _____ as a result of the processing methods used to manufacture it and therefore erodes faster, creating (iii) _____ cycle of erosion and replacement.

Blank (i)	Blank (ii)	Blank (iii)
an escalation	darker	an accelerated and expensive
a depletion	smaller-grained	an ineffective and unhygienic
a altercation	foul-smelling	a never-ending and inexplicable

39.   The human ability to recognize that the size of an object is _____, even as the distance between the person and object makes it appear to change in size, is called size constancy.

immutable
flexible
stable
abiding
uniform

40. Perception differs from sensation and refers not just to the reception of stimuli, but the _____ of those stimuli to determine what information can be gathered and how the information should be used.

insight
interpretation
translation
elucidation
adaptation

41. An example of operant conditioning is a commuter who _____, after several experiences, which route to his or her job takes the least amount of time, and adopts that route as a result of this learning.

assumes
theorizes
ascertains
disputes
validates

42. Psychologists refer to the ability to determine what information is important and what is background noise as signal detection, as it is the act of detecting what signals require or deserve focus and which can be _____.

unheeded
rejected
considered
abandoned
underestimated

43. Sensory adaptation occurs when a stimulus that is _____.when a subject first encounters it, eventually fades from notice, such as the sound of a ticking clock, or cooking smells in a room.

negligible
pronounced
significant
imperceptible
appreciable

44.   All vertebrate cardiovascular systems include a heart, a muscular pump that contracts to (i)
        _____.blood through the blood vessels. The upper chamber of the heart is the atrium, and is
        where blood enters the muscle. The lower chamber is the ventricle. When the ventricle (ii) _____.,
        blood is forced from the heart via an artery. The aorta is the main artery leaving the heart and bringing
        nutrients and oxygen out to the other organs. The pulmonary artery returns the oxygen-(iii)
        _____.blood to the heart so that it can be enriched with nutrients and sent back out into the body.

Blank (i)	Blank (ii)	Blank (iii)
pitch	constricts	squandered
propel	compresses	augmented
project	cinches	depleted

45.   While single celled organisms use the cell surface to (i) _____.nutrients from the world outside the
        system, and to release waste from the organism, multi-celled organisms require a circulatory system
        and medium of transport for nutrients. Sea-sponges, among the most (ii) _____.animals, take
        advantage of sea-water as a medium of transport, as the sea water flows in and out of the organism it
        delivers nutrients and removes waste.

Blank (i)	Blank (ii)
annex	primitive
procure	vestigial
relinquish	rudimentary

46.   Diabetes results from inadequate levels of insulin in the body. When not enough insulin is produced
        many physiological functions are compromised. The results includes vision (i) _____., decreased
        circulatory function, failures in the nervous system and kidney failure. The second most common cause
        of blindness in the United States is diabetes, which demonstrates how serious and (ii) _____.this
        condition is in the U.S.

Blank (i)	Blank (ii)
diminishing	pervasive
stagnation	circumscribed
impairment	capacious

47. In the human body two systems manage hormone release. The endocrine system is a (i) _____ of glands each of which (ii) _____ different hormones into the blood stream. Hormones pass through the blood to bring "messages" to different organs, which have hormone-receptors. The exocrine system, which is distinct from the endocrine system, an internal system, releases products outside of the body, including sweat and saliva.

Blank (i)
force
crux
cadre

Blank (ii)
disperse
secrete
beget

48. While single-celled organisms can (i) _____ nutrients directly from the environment, multicellular organisms have specialized structures for obtaining and breaking down the food that is the source of necessary nutrients. These digestive systems are composed of multiple functions that (ii) _____ food sources into processable liquid and extract nutrients. The process results in waste, which is expelled from the organism via another, related system.

Blank (i)
osmose
exude
cull

Blank (ii)
flux
deliquesce
coagulate

49. An Augustinian monk, Gregor Mendel, studied genetics by conducting experiments on garden peas, and in 1865 was the first scientist to propose the concept of _____ traits and the science of genetics.

bequeathed
inbred
maternal
acquired
heritable

50.   Robert Remark, a Polish embryologist, discovered that cells originated from the division of _____ cells and did not spontaneously appear.

inanimate
extant
living
surviving
mortal

51.   In 1665, Robert Hooke discovered the cell and established the _____ for the development of cell theory, and based on his discoveries, other scientists were able to develop new theories.

infrastructure
innovation
consequence
foundation
production

52.   It is not just the existence of multiple types of cells, but the _____ between these cells that allow a multi-cellular organism to function

communion
accord
synergy
intimacy
contention

53.   Rather than operate independently, cells in a multi-cellular organism are arranged into complex _____ of specialized cells that work together to complete complex functions.

cooperatives
aggregates
collectives
division
unanimity

54.   In 1915 Niels Bohr proposed a model of an atom that modified an earlier model. Based on quantum mechanics, the Bohr model is called a planetary model, as it shows electrons with a negative charge (i) _____ a nucleus, which has a positive charge. Bohr suggested a(n) (ii) _____ relationship between gravitational forces in the solar system and the electrical force between positively charged nucleus and negatively charged electrons.

Blank (i)
envelops
converges
orbits

Blank (ii)
analogous
homologous
retrogression

55.   An element is a(n) (i) _____ substance. It cannot be broken into other elements and has no component elements. There are 92 elements that occur in nature. When different elements are connected to create a new substance, the result is a compound, which is made of multiple, sometimes (ii) _____ elements, that are otherwise unrelated. Pure elements are rare as most matter exists in the form of compounds.

Blank (i)
unalloyed
adulterated
veritable

Blank (ii)
multifarious
homogenous
conglomerate

56.   In a(n) (i) _____ relationship, when one variable increases, the other decreases. The most (ii) _____ obvious example of this involves heating water. When a pan of water is placed over a heat source, as the temperature rises, liquid water begins to vaporize, thus reducing the mass of the water in the pan. In this case, as the variable temperature increases, the variable, mass, decreases.

Blank (i)
contradictory
conforming
inverse

Blank (ii)
familiar
proverbial
mundane

57.   While the consequences of criminal law cases may exceed those of civil law, especially in terms of financial reparations, the two function_____ to maintain social order.

perniciously
superciliously
redundantly
intractably
conjunctly

58.   The meteorologists of the world have recently found themselves working under the (i) _____ of political discourse. With environmental concerns suddenly on everybody's mind, these (ii) _____ scientists have been thrust into the vicious world of political partisanship. Although many of them have stepped up to the challenge admirably, it seems unfair to suddenly demand political insight from people previously focused exclusively on scientific pursuits.

Blank (i)
encumbrance
auspices
insight

Blank (ii)
reticent
ostentatious
conspiratorial

59.   In spite of the immense intellect, and sometimes outright genius, of the people working within it, the field of physics still faces many factors (i) _____ to its growth. As it turns out, the difficulty of accepting new ideas does not exist solely among the working-class population, but can be found in academia as well. Entrenched logic, petty careerism, and just plain (ii) _____are all as prevalent in the field of physics as they are in the conventional, nine-to-five world.

Blank (i)
correlated
antagonistic
supplanted

Blank (ii)
eminence
acquiescence
inscience

60. Fiona was simultaneously (i) _____ by the magic of dreams and turned off by their potential to turn into nightmares. She wondered what they revealed about the human psyche. They were so (ii) _____, yet there had to be some logical impetus for their genesis. She often read books on dream analysis in order to better understand this topic, but the more she read the more she suspected that the purported "experts" in the field were merely (iii) _____.

Blank (i)	Blank (ii)	Blank (iii)
enraptured	debonair	charlatans
vindicated	abstruse	solemn
denounced	gentile	guileless

61. Locating the (i) _____ organisms of the ocean has proven a daunting task. The ocean has more than 250 times the habitable volume as the land, leaving (ii) _____ amounts of space to cover. Even being able to locate viruses and phytoplankton, let alone being able to study their relationship to the environment, is a tremendous undertaking. But (iii) _____ understanding of marine life cannot be attained without knowing the role that microscopic organisms play in it.

Blank (i)	Blank (ii)	Blank (iii)
haughty	exorbitant	exhaustive
vituperative	coquettish	diminutive
enigmatic	ardent	reticent

62. Just the name "Biotechnology" evokes powerful images: the use of recombinant genes in genetic sequencing, applied immunology to fight diseases, and so on. But the lofty heading of "Biogerontology" includes many (i) _____that one wouldn't typically associate with advanced medicine. Both the brewing of alcohol and the development of agriculture involve manipulating biological systems to make products. Therefore, even without the scientific (ii) _____ of medical techniques, these "rough-and-tumble" jobs also fall under the heading of "Biotechnology."

Blank (i)	Blank (ii)
verisimilitudes	exactitude
denigrations	unsophistication
vocations	fallacy

63. Although its desolate landscapes and small population may make South Dakota seem a (i) _____ locale, it is actually one of the best places to start a business. High taxes in eastern states like New York and New Jersey can (ii) _____ even well-planned ventures. In contrast, South Dakota has some of the lowest taxes in the country.

Blank (i)
morbid
inhospitable
germane

Blank (ii)
foil
obviate
lampoon

64. Ghengis Khan is remembered as one of history's most _____ leaders; as founder of the Mongol Empire, he initiated the invasions that would ultimately lead to Mongol control of most of Eurasia.

rancorous
timorous
Disingenuous
Erratic
Belligerent

65. Women, though not (i) _____ genetic disorders generally, are far less likely than men to display symptoms of an X-linked hereditary disease such as hemophilia. In the case of hemophilia, for example, the woman's second, X chromosome acts as a kind of buffer; the normal gene is typically able to produce enough clotting factors to (ii) _____ any life-threatening bleeds.

Blank (i)
inclined to
intransigent towards
impervious to

Blank (ii)
mollify
forestall
engender

66. If the candidate's speech was intended to stir up (i) _____ feeling, he must have been sorely disappointed by the almost (ii) _____ effect it had on the audience. Although it was refreshing to see a politician (iii) _____ inflammatory taglines in favor of reasoned argument, his speech was simply too long to hold the audience's attention.

Blank (i)	Blank (ii)	Blank (iii)
rancorous	incendiary	eschew
partisan	noxious	preclude
indigenous	soporific	abhor

67. The findings of multiple social psychology studies suggest that humans are much more (i) _____ than we like to admit. Although we tend to think of our opinions and beliefs as highly personal and deeply-rooted, the truth is that they are greatly influenced by our surroundings. In some cases, we are even willing to (ii) _____ the evidence of our own senses in the interests of conformity; in the Asch experiments, participants routinely misjudged the length of a line in order to (iii) _____ the majority judgment.

Blank (i)	Blank (ii)	Blank (iii)
tractable	vituperate	abide by
fatuous	repudiate	preclude
dogmatic	garner	quibble with

68. No doubt because of its potential hazards, we tend to think of radiation as something out of the ordinary; in truth, however, radiation is essentially _____, and it is therefore impossible to avoid low-level exposure.

ineffable
ubiquitous
nebulous
quiescent
foolproof

69.   Invasive species constitute a serious threat to (i) _____ plants and animals, whether by preying on them directly or competing with them for resources. The emerald ash borer has had a particularly (ii) _____ effect on the environment; as its name implies, it attacks and kills all varieties of ash trees, and it is spreading throughout the United States at an alarming rate.

Blank (i)	Blank (ii)
inveterate	deleterious
pugnacious	covert
indigenous	perfidious

70.   The English teacher was impressed by his newest student's _____ observations; on her first day in class, she commented on several aspects of the novel that her classmates had overlooked.

urbane
pedantic
trenchant
equivocal
loquacious

71.   The death of Hu Yaobang, a Party leader committed to economic and social reforms, was the (i) _____ that caused the now famous Tiananmen Square protests. The demonstrations, which lasted seven weeks and were primarily non-violent, culminated in the government's brutal massacre of hundreds, if not thousands, of protestors - a (ii) _____ abuse of government power that resulted in widespread (iii) _____.

Blank (i)	Blank (ii)	Blank (iii)
catalyst	redoubtable	encomium
imbroglio	heinous	sanctimony
antidote	dubious	opprobrium

72.   Prior to the nineteenth century, female ballet dancers were effectively barred from lead roles due to their (i) _____ corsets, hoops, and high heels. With the invention of the pointed shoe, however, all of this changed; ballet dancers came to be seen as ethereal creatures capable of floating effortlessly across the stage. Ballets consequently began to feature stories of nymphs and spirits that showcased the (ii) _____ costumes and (iii) _____ bodies of nineteenth-century ballerinas.

Blank (i)	Blank (ii)	Blank (iii)
cumbersome	dulcet	brittle
maladroit	meretricious	supine
disheveled	diaphanous	lithe

73.   Perhaps not surprisingly, a recent study suggests that teens in the United States spend a _____ amount of money on clothes; in fact, apparel accounts for roughly 20 percent of all teen spending.

conspicuous
temperate
nebulous
ignominious
impecunious

74.   Although folklore regards a green sky as a (i) _____ of tornadoes, the belief is not backed by scientific evidence. In fact, tornadoes are one of the more unpredictable forms of severe weather; although radar can detect signs indicating a possible tornado, such data generally requires eyewitness (ii) _____.

Blank (i)	Blank (ii)
propagation	reciprocity
incursion	approbation
harbinger	corroboration

75.   Those who are familiar with Shakespeare's plays no doubt see Richard III as a murderous (i) _____ who killed his two young nephews in order to claim the throne for himself. Some modern historians, however, believe that the evidence against Richard is (ii) _____ at best, and suggest that Shakespeare may have had politically compelling reasons for (iii) _____ his character.

Blank (i)	Blank (ii)	Blank (iii)
iconoclast	quotidian	renovating
mendicant	tenuous	commemorating
reprobate	whimsical	maligning

76.   The children grew _____ when cold temperatures forced them to remain inside.

boorish
phlegmatic
gregarious
restive
feckless

77.   The most successful companies can have humble – even (i) _____ - beginnings; that Sony's first product was an ineffective rice cooker surely proves that (ii) _____ is nearly as important as vision when trying to get a business off the ground.

Blank (i)	Blank (ii)
mundane	tenacity
frugal	presumption
bogus	sophistry

78. Victimology at times ventures into highly (i) _____ areas, such as victim precipitation, which occurs
     when a victim attracts the attention of an attacker through (ii) _____ behavior of some sort.
     Although studies that center on the victim's identity and habits ultimately aim to reduce crime, to
     some, the terminology used in such research does little besides blame the victim and implicitly (iii)
     _____ the crime.

Blank (i)	Blank (ii)	Blank (iii)
salacious	timorous	condone
propitious	brash	provoke
contentious	fulsome	rescind

79. Monteverdi's L'Orfeo enjoys its (i) _____ reputation in part because it is regarded as the first fully
     developed opera. Yet due credit must also be given to both the score and the libretto, which retells the
     (ii) _____ tale of Orpheus's journey to the underworld to restore his beloved Eurydice to life.

Blank (i)	Blank (ii)
renowned	droll
incongruous	poignant
unscathed	maudlin

80. The (i) _____ nature of the sloth is well documented; its very name is a reference to the Biblical sin of
     spiritual and physical apathy. Unlike the average (ii) _____, however, the sloth has a compelling
     reason to (iii) _____ physical activity; the sloth's diet consists almost entirely of leaves, which
     provide little in the way of energy or nutrition, forcing the sloth to conserve its strength.

Blank (i)	Blank (ii)	Blank (iii)
fulsome	virago	abstain from
lugubrious	libertine	inveigh against
phlegmatic	sluggard	wean themselves off

81.   Though we were charmed by the (i) _____ waters of the Mediterranean, the highlight of our trip to
       Greece was undoubtedly the chance to visit the Parthenon. Photos cannot adequately capture the
       grandeur of this (ii) _____ relic from ancient times, so we found ourselves stunned into silence when
       confronted by its stately columns and imposing pediments.

Blank (i)
pellucid
turbid
quiescent

Blank (ii)
portentous
august
irrevocable

82.   It is hardly surprising that questions concerning the nature and behavior of light have _____ some of
       the most brilliant thinkers throughout history; depending on how it is studied, light exhibits the
       properties of either a wave or a particle.

placated
confounded
fettered
implicated
enervated

83.   An eye for seemingly (i) _____ details can make all the difference in marketing a product. Color, for
       example, can have (ii) _____ but powerful effects on a person's mood if not used carefully. Yellow
       runs the risk of being overpowering, but its undeniably eye-catching intensity can be an effective tool
       for a (iii) _____ businessman; Harry N. Allan, who first brought the taxicab to the United States,
       painted his cars yellow for precisely this reason.

Blank (i)
disparate
spurious
trifling

Blank (ii)
inadvertent
nugatory
salutary

Blank (iii)
sagacious
impecunious
officious

84. The _____ with which he ate appalled the other guests, who prided themselves on their impeccable
     table manners.

efficacy
decorum
adroitness
temperance
alacrity

85. Petra's one-time importance as a key stop on a trade route is reflected in its unique and beautiful
     architecture; although the so-called "Great Temple " was almost certainly built by an Arab tribe known
     as the Nabataeans, its style reveals a _____ of cultural influences - its columns, for example, draw on
     both the Corinthian and Suleiman styles.

travesty
dearth
adulteration
plethora
imprecation

86. In order to _____ the hypothesized age of a given fossil, scientists rely on their knowledge of the
     radioactive decay rates of various isotopes.

correlate
discern
substantiate
gainsay
palliate

87. While the study of viruses is important in and of itself, it must be noted that it also has potential (i) _____ for other areas of medicine. For example, a handful of otherwise innocuous viruses may (ii) _____ the development of certain forms of cancer; the Epstein-Barr virus has so far been linked to Hodgkin's lymphoma, Burkitt's lymphoma, nasopharyngeal carcinoma, and central nervous system lymphomas associated with HIV.

Blank (i)
proscriptions
exigencies
ramifications

Blank (ii)
precipitate
attenuate
truncate

88. Although incest is now (i) _____ to many, if not most, societies, a surprisingly large number of cultures have at one time or another permitted it. Indeed, brother-sister marriage was virtually (ii) _____ within the ancient Egyptian royal family, where it was used to ensure that the bloodline remained _____.

Blank (i)	Blank (ii)	Blank (iii)
venial	condoned	omnipotent
abhorred	mandated	immaculate
ancillary	rectified	empyreal

89. While most people are aware of the existence of vestigial structures like the appendix, far fewer realize that humans also retain some reflexes and behaviors that, though (i) _____ now, would have proven valuable to the organisms from which we evolved. Goose bumps, for example, cause whatever fur an animal has to stand on end, thereby making it appear larger and a more (ii) _____ opponent when faced with a potential predator.

Blank (i)
superfluous
apocryphal
exiguous

Blank (ii)
impassive
formidable
obsequious

90. Although The Picture of Dorian Gray was (i) _____ at the time of its publication as a (ii) _____ account of a man's descent into moral depravity, it is now regarded as a classic work of English literature. In fact, the book's history underscores how the current social climate can (iii) _____ the true value of a piece of art.

Blank (i)	Blank (ii)	Blank (iii)
vaunted	histrionic	obfuscate
reviled	insipid	emblazon
expunged	lurid	atrophy

91. Contrary to a popular myth, the _____ pinks and oranges of a sunset are at their most brilliant in areas with relatively unpolluted air.

fervid
plangent
crepuscular
lambent
winsome

92. The governor signed the bill into law despite widespread and (i) _____ objections, leading some to question whether he truly had the people's best interests at heart. In response to such criticisms, the governor merely stated that the new laws, however (ii) _____ in the short term, were ultimately necessary.

Blank (i)	Blank (ii)
bombastic	unpalatable
moribund	imminent
vociferous	execrable

93. In 2010, California approved a cap-and-trade program that aims to reduce the greenhouse gas emissions of California-based businesses. But while most people agree that action must be taken to (i) _____ the worst effects of climate change, some companies feel these particular demands are too (ii) _____ to meet. Makers of concrete are particularly (iii) _____ of the new regulations; because the release of carbon dioxide is central to the production of concrete, the new law could have devastating effects for businesses that specialize in this.

Blank (i)
forestall
descry
propitiate

Blank (ii)
onerous
meretricious
amorphous

Blank (iii)
cognizant
wary
devoid

94. The Romantic notion of "the sublime" has its origins in the eighteenth-century fascination with the natural world in all its forms; the term was used to describe landscapes so awe-inspiring that they simultaneously terrified and _____ those who saw them.

perturbed
eviscerated
transcended
galvanized
beguiled

95. Although we tend to think of our judgments of others as (i) _____ observations, the reality is that a variety of unconscious beliefs and biases affect our opinions. For example, we so expect a person's physical appearance to (ii) _____ his overall intelligence and morality that attractive people are more likely to receive good grades in school and land a well-paying job.

Blank (i)
dispassionate
chary
momentous

Blank (ii)
ascribe to
purport to
jibe with

96. The average person is likely familiar with only three phases of matter - solid, liquid, and gas - and would no doubt be _____ to learn of the bizarre states of matter, such as super fluids and Bose-Einstein condensates, that can occur at extremely low temperatures.

contrite
saturnine
nonplussed
dispirited
livid

97. It did not take the new members long to see that the group was (i) _____ its leadership was disorganized and (ii) _____ and virtually all efforts at community outreach had ceased. They hoped, however, that their own enthusiasm would not only revive the organization but also (iii) _____ renewed outside interest in its cause.

Blank (i)	Blank (ii)	Blank (iii)
chimerical	frowzy	perpetrate
superannuated	torpid	foster
moribund	stringent	convoke

98. Even the most (i) _____ of glances at one of Vincent van Gogh's paintings will give the viewer some idea of his highly distinctive style. His use of bold brushstrokes and (ii) _____ colors give his art an unusual emotional intensity - an intensity that can be somewhat disconcerting when one remembers his (iii) _____ struggle with mental illness.

Blank (i)	Blank (ii)	Blank (iii)
cursory	incarnadine	iniquitous
jaundiced	funereal	harrowing
perspicacious	dynamic	affected

99.   The jagged peaks and _____ drops of the Himalayas are signs of their relative youth; older mountains tend to be smaller and more rounded as a result of erosion.

overweening
notorious
surreptitious
precipitous
nascent

100.   Although their (i) _____ beauty suggests extreme fragility, butterflies have developed a number of practical defenses against predators and other dangers. Some species advertise their (ii) _____ taste with bright colors and memorable patterns in the hopes that a predator will not make the same mistake twice, while others attempt to (iii) _____ their enemies with misleading eye-shaped spots on their wings.

Blank (i)	Blank (ii)	Blank (iii)
tremulous	insidious	maim
inordinate	elusive	placate
mincing	fulsome	confound

101.   Although the (i) _____ against murder is universal, the definition of the crime is highly (ii) _____. A strict adherence to Buddhist teachings, for example, would most likely lead one to condemn even killing in self-defense, which is generally tolerated in modern society.

Blank (i)	Blank (ii)
litigation	contentious
vituperation	fallacious
proscription	inclusive

102. Although all parents expect some degree of (i) _____ obedience, those that carry their demands may inadvertently hinder their child's development. Children who grow up in a household where absolute (ii) _____ parental authority is the norm are often not given a chance to exercise their own judgment, and may therefore have low-self esteem and a (iii) _____ sense of self.

Blank (i)	Blank (ii)	Blank (iii)
filial	propensity for	tenuous
reciprocal	intransigence towards	mercurial
scrupulous	deference to	dissolute

103. Although the majority of urban legends are no doubt _____ their doubtful origins do not seem to have any effect on their ability to captivate listeners.

hyperbolic
ephemeral
judicious
prurient
apocryphal

104. Much to the (i) _____ of consumers, modern technology has allowed businesses to advertise more effectively - and more (ii) _____ than ever; the average city-dweller is now exposed to somewhere between 3,000 and 5,000 ads every day. The constant (iii) _____ of marketing is so frustrating that 43 percent of cell phone users say they would willingly pay more for a cell phone service that blocks such messages.

Blank (i)	Blank (ii)	Blank (iii)
edification	consummately	dearth
trepidation	obtrusively	parlance
disgruntlement	nefariously	barrage

105. Cirrus clouds, which form high in the atmosphere and are known for their wispy, _____ appearance, are actually composed of ice crystals rather than water droplets.

halcyon
sinuous
gossamer
variegated
lambent

106. Those unfamiliar with her (i) _____ sense of humor tended to take her words at face value, and were sometimes repelled by her apparent inability to speak seriously of any subject. For those in the know, however, her (ii) _____ remarks were endlessly entertaining.

Blank (i)
flippant
raucous
erudite

Blank (ii)
jocular
iconoclastic
equivocal

107. According to the theory of natural selection, traits that prove particularly _____ have a greater chance of being passed on to future generations, because the individuals that possess these traits are more likely to survive long enough to mate.

innocuous
expedient
salient
titillating
prolific

108. Although the Salem witch trials remain a (i) _____ passage of American history, there is no shortage of speculation as to their cause. Although the hallucinations purportedly experienced by the victims may have resulted from something as simple as moldy bread, it seems likely that socio-economic tensions and the (ii) _____ religious climate created an atmosphere in which mass hysteria could (iii) _____.

Blank (i)	Blank (ii)	Blank (iii)
clandestine	austere	convene
enigmatic	vitriolic	fester
infamous	pristine	languish

109. Cyrano de Bergerac, as he is portrayed in Rostand's play, is something of a (i) _____. For all his swagger and (ii) _____ words, he remains a deeply sympathetic character, no doubt because at heart he is simply an insecure man tormented by unrequited love.

Blank (i)
archetype
paradox
cliche

Blank (ii)
licentious
iconoclastic
bombastic

110. His decision to become a middle-school drama teacher surprised those who were familiar with his considerable talent and (i) _____ interest in performing. In response to the queries of his friends, he said that felt it was (ii) _____ him to do something about the (iii) _____ state of arts education in the public schools.

Blank (i)	Blank (ii)	Blank (iii)
manifest	inimical to	banal
inordinate	munificent of	abysmal
perfunctory	incumbent upon	odious

111. Although the differences are no doubt (i) _____ to the casual listener, various studies have that men and women do not use language in precisely the same way. Men, for example, are far more likely to compliment women than vice versa, perhaps due to deeply ingrained cultural attitudes that condemn as (ii) _____ any romantically assertive woman.

Blank (i)
pertinent
blatant
indiscernible

Blank (ii)
garish
brazen
capricious

112. 3M is an extremely diversified company, with businesses dealing in health care, office supplies, display and graphics, electronics and communications, industry and transportation, and security and personal protection all falling under its _____.

aegis
vagaries
covenant
opus
tutelage

113. When thinking about the vast (i) _____ of the universe, it is hard to (ii) _____ that there could be more than one galaxy like the Milky Way, which is home to millions of stars, but according to scientists there are an untold number of galaxies, all moving through the universe at different (iii) _____.

Blank (i)	Blank (ii)	Blank (iii)
length	fathom	velocities and trajectories
darkness	explain	ways and means
reaches	measure	angles and dimensions

114. Some scholars (i) _____ that the works of William Shakespeare were in fact written by a(n) (ii) _____ of authors, rather than a single man. But, they have a difficult time identifying any possible suspects, figuring out how many there were or explaining how so many people could write in such a(n) (iii) _____.

Blank (i)	Blank (ii)	Blank (iii)
declaim	coterie	cohesive style
assume	menagerie	flamboyant manner
contend	gild	complicated time

115. Automobiles sold in the United States have either a manual or automatic transmission. If the car is a manual, that means the driver has to shift through a (i) _____ of gears to accelerate, while an automatic car will shift on its own with no (ii) _____ from the driver. It is fair to say driving an automatic takes (iii) _____, but most people can learn to drive a manual with little trouble.

Blank (i)	Blank (ii)	Blank (iii)
gamut	contrivance	less coordination
sequence	assistance	a long time
filigree	reliance	more stability

116. Gazelles are known to be fast as well as (i) _____; this often leads people to (ii) _____ dance and ballet performers with these graceful creatures of the savanna.

Blank (i)	Blank (ii)
erratic	associate
lithe	trivialize
diaphanous	defer

117. Good financial (i) _____ is required to run a small business, and if you are not (ii) _____in the ways of accounting, you should consider hiring a professional.

Blank (i)
vitiate
acumen
credence

Blank (ii)
pliant
learned
frenetic

118. The study of metallurgy involves the mining and processing of metal (i) _____, as well as the mixing of different types of metals to form (ii) _____.

Blank (i)
magma
ore
treacle

Blank (ii)
composites
deposits
striates

119. Blinking is an involuntary movement that occurs many times a day, and most times people are not even _____ of the fact that they do it so often.

reticent
foretold
cognizant
belied
unctuous

120. Monarch butterflies have a very long and often (i) _____ migration route that can often take them several months depending on their (ii) _____ in North America.

Blank (i)
vicarious
fractious
precarious

Blank (ii)
volition
origin
polarity

121. Most people in North America are more familiar with grey squirrels, but in some regions and smaller, _____ areas, black squirrels thrive in abundance.

variegated
razed
homogenized
localized
denigrated

122. "Shooting stars" are meteors, hunks of rocks that (i) _____ through space, that burn up in the Earth's atmosphere in a streak that can often be seen by the naked eye; meteorites are pieces of meteors that aren't completely (ii) _____, and fall all the way to the ground.

Blank (i)
hurtle
waft
droll

Blank (ii)
collated
extirpated
serrated

123. The people's (i) _____ toward their repressive government increased when they heard that a series of long-promised reforms were (ii) _____. The parliament had been suspended indefinitely, meaning that no changes would be made for the foreseeable future.

Blank (i)
revulsion
fidelity
rancor

Blank (ii)
saprophagous
moribund
nascent

124. The former dictator's (i) _____ was legendary, although it was only after he was deposed, the full extent of his wealth became know - huge mansions spread across the country, and a (ii) _____ of luxury goods.

Blank (i)
prowess
cupidity
prudishness

Blank (ii)
paucity
surfeit
postulate

125. Judge Gordon was known for his _____ in upholding the law; although his rulings sometimes went against his personal preferences, they were always in keeping with legal precedent.

turpitude
probity
speciousness
torpor
urbanity

126. Our group worked _____ on the account; for months many of us got to work early and left late, and some even took work home.

ambiguously
exultantly
formidably
imperturbably
assiduously

127. We were appalled by the waiter's _____; when we complained that our food came cold, he told us that it was our fault for ordering an unusual dish.

effrontery
pusillanimity
dexterity
circumspection
asperity

128. My seat mate was so _____ that I could neither sleep nor read through the entire flight.

lethargic
rapacious
irascible
loquacious
indigent

129.   Medieval European rulers often tried to legitimize their rule by (i) _____ ties to the ancient Roman Empire. Although actual ties were tenuous, this strategy engendered the German emperor adopting the (ii) _____ title of "Holy Roman Emperor".

Blank (i)
rending
alleviating
espousing

Blank (ii)
ludicrous
grandiose
gregarious

130.   Walt's presentation was very _____; it helped clarify some difficult aspects of our group's goals for the remainder of the project.

lucid
malevolent
meretricious
obscure
bewildering

This page is intentionally left blank

Chapter **4**

Introduction to Sentence Equivalence

Sentence Equivalence questions your ability to interpret and understand what you read, and also your ability to use vocabulary in context. Each Sentence Equivalence question will consist of a sentence with a single blank. You will be asked to choose the two words from among six that produce complete sentences with the most similar meanings.

The passages used for Sentence Equivalence questions will be drawn from a variety of topics, including the physical, biological and social sciences, the arts and the humanities, business and everyday life. As with other types of questions for the Verbal Reasoning component, you need not be an expert on the topics covered in Sentence Equivalence questions too. You will, however, need to read the passage carefully enough to understand what is being said, and be able to complete the sentence grammatically. All Sentence Equivalence questions will follow the same multiple choice format. You will be given a sentence with a single blank, and will be given 6 options to fill in the blank. You will need to choose the TWO options that produce a grammatically correct sentence with the most similar meaning

What does a Sentence Equivalence question look like?

Sentence Equivalence questions will always be based off a single sentence. The sentence will have a single blank. You will be asked to read the sentence and get a feel for what two words from among six given will produce sentences with the most similar meaning. Below is an example of what a Sentence Equivalence question will look like on the GRE General Test:

Select the two answer choices that, when used to complete the sentence, fit the meaning of the sentence as a whole and produce completed sentences that are alike in meaning.

1.   Under Stalin, the Soviet state showed many of the same BLANK tendencies of the Tsarist government it had replaced; dissent of any kind was stifled and political authority was centralized.

   [A]   liberalizing

   [B]   despotic

   [C]   vicious

   [C]   corrupt

   [D]   oligarchic

   [E]   autocratic

Answer Key

The answers to the above question are B. despotic and F. autocratic.

What skills do Sentence Equivalence questions test?

Like Text Completion questions, Sentence Equivalence questions test your ability to understand what you are reading and reason from incomplete information. However, Sentence Equivalence questions focus more on the meaning of a single sentence, so you'll need to be able to differentiate how different words complete the sentence. Some key skills that are tested include your ability to

- reason based on incomplete information

- understand the meaning of sentences

- understand high level vocabulary

- apply vocabulary in context

Key Facts about Sentence Equivalence questions

- Questions will be based off a single short sentence

- For each passage, you will need to fill in a single blank using the 6 options provided

- Passages will be on a variety of topics including the physical, biological and social sciences, the arts and the humanities, business and everyday life

- Questions will be answerable based on the information in the passage alone and your ability to apply vocabulary

- You will need to choose TWO options to fill in a single blank. Look for the two words that will produce two distinct, coherent, and grammatically correct sentences with similar meanings

Strategies for Sentence Equivalence Questions

Sentence Equivalence questions are the least time-intensive question type you will see on the Verbal Reasoning component. Time budgeting is important for every component of the test, however, assuming that you have managed your time well for other types of questions, you should have plenty to time to give the necessary attention to Sentence Equivalence questions. Like Text Completion questions, it is important that you read Sentence Equivalence questions with care. Do not skim Sentence Equivalence questions, since it is important that you understand exactly what the sentence means. Missing a key word in a Sentence Equivalence can spell disaster since the focus for these questions is very narrow. Given that each question is based on a single sentence, even a careful reading should not take very long. If you find yourself taking any more than a minute or so on a Sentence Equivalence, you should skip to another question and come back to it later if you have time.

As with the other types of questions on the Verbal Reasoning portion, do not let the subject matter of the passage throw you off - your ability to correctly answer these questions is independent of any expertise you may possess in the subject area of the passage. When answering Sentence Equivalence questions, you will need to be able to quickly assess the meaning of a sentence based on incomplete information, and have enough command of vocabulary to choose the words that will be the best fit to complete the sentence. You WILL NOT need to make any judgement about whether the passage is true or false.

The key skills for Sentence Equivalence questions are understanding the meaning of specific sentences and how individual words shape meaning. As you read the sentence, don't give the topic too much thought - focus on what the sentence means. Be sure to attend to important words that signal emphasis or qualification as these will help you decide which words will be the best fit for the blank. As with Text Completion, your vocabulary will play a role in your ability to do well on Sentence Equivalence questions. However, keep in mind that you will always be using words in context, so you won't necessarily need to know their exact meaning or dictionary definition. Also, remember that your task is to produce two sentences with the most similar meaning, not to find the two words with the most similar meaning.

- Read the passage carefully - do not skim

- Read the sentence carefully - do not skim

- Attend to key words that for sections of the passage that either closely match or negate the definition of one of the word options

- Apply vocabulary in context

What follows are some more specific strategies for answering Sentence Equivalence questions. In the next chapter, you'll have a chance to put your skills to the test through several practice questions and learn how to hone them in the answers and explanations that follow.

Review Vocabulary

Previous versions of the GRE featured sections that were specifically geared toward vocabulary. The GRE General Test no longer features these sections, but as has been noted previously, vocabulary is still very important. This is especially so for Text Completion and Sentence Equivalence questions, where you will need to have some idea of what some "big" words mean in order to fill in the appropriate blanks. Note that Sentence Equivalence questions focus on the meaning of the completed sentence more than on the meaning of any individual word, so you can often get away with having a ballpark understanding of what a word means. Nonetheless, anything that you can do to strengthen your vocabulary prior to the test will be helpful, since the test assumes a fairly high level vocabulary. If you are not confident of your vocabulary, do what you can to improve it as preparation for the test (this will serve you well in graduate school as well). Again, there are many cases when you will not need to know a precise definition of a word, but you will need to have a general sense of what it means. There are several things you can do to improve your vocabulary for the test:

- Review lists of common "GRE words" such as the one included in this book

- Use a vocabulary builder

- Get a sense of key Greek or Latin root words and what they mean - many words in English are based on Greek or Latin words, and knowing the meaning of a few key Greek or Latin words can help you figure out the meanings of numerous English words

Read the Sentence Carefully

Before you try to fill in any blank, read the sentence carefully. Sentence Equivalence questions focus on the meaning of sentences, so you'll need to get a clear sense of what the sentence means without the blank filled in to get a clear sense of what words will effectively complete it.

Pay Special Attention to Significant Words

As with Text Completion questions, you should pay close attention to pivotal words in the sentence in Sentence Equivalence questions too. Key words can give tremendous insight into the meaning of the sentence and provide strong indicators of what word you will need to choose to complete the sentence correctly. Words like "although", "despite", "moreover" or "therefore" which either emphasize or qualify something that has been said are often especially significant, so look out for them and be sensitive to how they modify the meaning of the sentence.

Be Careful Not to Make Your Choice Solely on the Meaning of Words

It may sound counter-intuitive, but sometimes two words with very similar meanings will not necessarily produce sentences of similar meanings. When answering Sentence Completion questions, you might be tempted to simply select the two words from among the options that have the most similar meaning, and use them to answer the question. This is a bad strategy for two reasons. In the first place, sometimes there will be more than one pair of words that have similar meanings. Without focusing on the meaning of the sentence, you might choose the wrong pair, since you need to produce two grammatically correct, coherent sentences with similar meanings and not just find words that have similar meanings. The second reason is more counter-intuitive; however, sometimes the two words with the most similar meanings will not produce the two sentences with the most similar meanings. Keep this in mind and always focus on the meaning of the sentence, rather than on the meaning of the words you are choosing to complete it.

Try to fill in the blank with your own word before you look at the answer choices

As with Text Completion questions, you can try to think of words that will fill in the blank to complete the sentence and then compare them to the options given to see if you can find any similar words. Sometimes you'll be able to see words that obviously correspond to those you have already thought of to fill in the blanks; other times, you'll be able to eliminate words with opposite meanings. Either of these options will be helpful to you as you try to answer the question.

Always check your work

As with Text Completion questions, be sure that you always fill in the options that you choose to complete the sentence to make certain that your choices produce coherent, grammatically correct sentences with similar meanings. Remember that you need to satisfy all of these requirements in your answer.

Use Process of Elimination

Process of elimination is ALWAYS useful in answering any type of multiple choice question, and Sentence Equivalence is no exception. Unless the answer is immediately obvious to you, you should always be looking to narrow your choices by getting rid of potential answers that don't fit, or don't make sense. When using process of elimination for Sentence Equivalence questions, always keep in mind what the goals of the question are. You need to find the two words that will produce two distinct sentences that are coherent, grammatically correct, and have similar meanings. If a word doesn't make sense in context, you can dismiss it. If a word doesn't fit grammatically into the sentence, you can dismiss it. Keep this in mind as you answer Sentence Equivalence questions, since it will help you eliminate inappropriate answer choices.

This page is intentionally left blank

Chapter 5

Practice Questions for Sentence Equivalence

1. Although the theory of the conservation of mass was not stated clearly until 1789, it had many _____ in the history of the physical sciences.

    A originators

    B derivatives

    C forerunners

    D antecedents

    E imitators

    F descendents

2. Einstein's discovery of general relativity is a major turning point in the history of physics and _____ a full century of further research.

    A stimulated

    B dampened

    C abetted

    D motivated

    E debilitated

    F vitalized

3.   Determinism, the notion that reality is independent of how we question or observe it, is the only
     conclusion that can be reasonably _____ from the classical form of Newtonian physics.

A	imputed
B	drawn
C	ascertained
D	calculated
E	derived
F	assumed

4.   Chemical thermodynamics _____ measurements of thermodynamic properties and the application
     of mathematical methods to the study of chemistry.

A	entails
B	subsumes
C	constitutes
D	contains
E	involves
F	embodies

5.   In accomplishing the seemingly impossible, the young woman was _____ by her desire to impress
     her parents.

A	inhibited
B	sedated
C	motivated
D	influenced
E	stymied
F	adjudicated

6. The sheer depth of space that must be traversed in order to locate even basic truths about the origins of our Universe has rendered _____ reasoning as one of the most effective way to shirk our empirical handicap.

    A inverse

    B deliberate

    C deductive

    D inferable

    E observable

    F obvious

7. The pervasive institutionalization of the notion that beauty must be suffered for has crippled the didactic efficacy of modern media and _____ the self-confidence of a whole generation of children.

    A subverted

    B undermined

    C initiated

    D rectified

    E invigorated

    F objectified

8. The differences in symptoms between the autism spectrum disorders and the anxiety conditions (such as obsessive compulsive disorder) are often so _____ that a patient can go years without receiving a proper diagnosis.

    A inconspicuous

    B pervasive

    C harmless

    D debilitating

    E subtle

    F extravagant

9. He watched the peripheral artery bypass through the observation window and marveled at the doctor's
    _____, which justified the already-tremendous amounts of audaciousness necessary to perform such
    a procedure.

    [A] aggression

    [B] reticence

    [C] proficiency

    [D] contempt

    [E] delusion

    [F] expertise

10. I asked her to stop _____ me all the time about fixing the faucet in the spare room bathroom.

    [A] hounding

    [B] bearing

    [C] ferreting

    [D] badgering

    [E] weaseling

    [F] remonstrating

11. Gang related crime was _____ in that area; even the police were wary about entering after dark.

    [A] epidemic

    [B] endemic

    [C] curtailed

    [D] governable

    [E] exuberant

    [F] prevalent

12.   The scent of freshly baked bread _____ into the room from the bakery below.

   A   drifted

   B   wafted

   C   coasted

   D   transmitted

   E   poised

   F   inured

13.   The evening's _____ rays were enchanting to behold as they lit the horizon with their amazing display of colour.

   A   twilight

   B   diurnal

   C   crepuscular

   D   noontide

   E   enlightened

   F   modicum

14.   It is quite remarkable to see a book in such _____ condition; I've never seen a 17th-century first edition of that high standard before.

   A   sanitary

   B   untarnished

   C   purified

   D   pristine

   E   immaculate

   F   adulterated

15.   In all respects, the designs were unpopular with the masses, they were both _____ and unpractical.

   [A]   sophisticated

   [B]   ill-bred

   [C]   clumsy

   [D]   gauche

   [E]   butterfingered

   [F]   couth

16.   In spite of his apparent knowledge of historical figures, Henry was a/an _____ when it came to well-known French Impressionists.

   [A]   dilettante

   [B]   unskilled

   [C]   amateur

   [D]   dabbling

   [E]   connoisseur

   [F]   proficient

17.   You could see why Annette was his muse; she had a healthy complexion and a/an _____ mane of golden tresses that cascaded down her back.

   [A]   barren

   [B]   profuse

   [C]   elaborate

   [D]   plenteous

   [E]   pretentious

   [F]   luxuriant

18. Rows of breathtakingly beautiful and _____ marble columns stretched the length of the basilica, watching over the 15th-century church's exceptional mosaic floor.

   A   clement

   B   ornate

   C   embroidered

   D   baroque

   E   dowdy

   F   garish

19. Despite its _____ dimensions, the office space was still undersized for our needs.

   A   capacious

   B   abundance

   C   expansive

   D   brimming

   E   minute

   F   discrepant

20. The marketing team _____ a new campaign to boost sales.

   A   connived

   B   contrived

   C   devised

   D   schemed

   E   blueprints

   F   casted

21.   It is known that many firms engage in misleading and often _____ accounting practices to inflate their short-term profits.

   A   counterfeit

   B   infamous

   C   fraudulent

   D   villainess

   E   dubious

   F   slanderous

22.   Due to recession, companies have learnt to be _____ with their marketing budgets and not spend outlandishly.

   A   gluttonous

   B   frugal

   C   altruistic

   D   lavish

   E   parsimonious

   F   miserly

23.   Archaeologists have found evidence that _____ tribes made baskets for collecting and storing food.

   A   old-fashioned

   B   primitive

   C   obsolete

   D   trampled

   E   antiquated

   F   archaic

24.   There was great public outrage when the _____ publication appeared in the media talking about the existence of child slavery in first world countries.

   A   quarrelsome

   B   controversial

   C   metaphysical

   D   doubtful

   E   polemic

   F   cantankerous

25.   Socialists often decry the _____ excesses of most capitalist societies.

   A   materialistic

   B   nonconforming

   C   indolent

   D   capitalism

   E   Victorian

   F   bourgeois

26.   Brazil and Argentina discussed the importance of gathering genetic information from the _____ tribes that live in the Amazonas region.

   A   homegrown

   B   inherited

   C   alien

   D   indigenous

   E   aboriginal

   F   inbred

27. The economic _____ between first world countries and third world countries have increased since the
     1950s.

     [A] disparities

     [B] burrow

     [C] disagreeable

     [D] hole

     [E] animosity

     [F] discrepancies

28. After such a lengthy illness, her complexion was still _____; she obviously needed a few more days of
     repose.

     [A] hearty

     [B] salubrious

     [C] bilious

     [D] albino

     [E] vigorous

     [F] sallow

29. The effects of urban gentrification is an ongoing tale of winners and losers; some residents benefit from
     the _____ of business investment and improved school quality that come with the
     improvements in neighborhoods, but other residents are displaced as rents increase and property taxes
     rise.

     [A] profusion

     [B] abridgement

     [C] ardor

     [D] parapet

     [E] accretion

     [F] culmination

30. The Internet provides a window into cultures that may be unfamiliar from the ones in which we live; a quick Internet search can provide _____ into how people from other cultures live, how they interact with one another, and what is important to them.

   [A] perspicacity

   [B] erudition

   [C] sagacity

   [D] sapience

   [E] apotheosis

   [F] proclivity

31. Technology has led to many changes in the time spent on household responsibilities; with the adoption of appliances such as microwaves, washing machines, and vacuum cleaners into the home, the time spent on household tasks have _____ tremendously compared to the substantial time spent on household duties a century ago.

   [A] bated

   [B] minified

   [C] masticated

   [D] attenuated

   [E] impinged

   [F] augmented

32. The human body's immune system is a powerful biological process that is responsible for fighting off thousands of harmful organisms; when the immune system is working properly, the body is protected from dangerous bacteria, but when it is impaired the body is vulnerable to a _____ of dangerous, disease-carrying microbes.

   [A] plethora

   [B] surfeit

   [C] legion

   [D] consanguinity

   [E] peculation

   [F] extolment

33. A microscope contains one or more lenses that magnify the image of the organism placed on its focal plane; depending on the power of the lens, the microscope can allow people to _____ view the cells of organisms with little to no effort.

  A mendaciously

  B salubriously

  C adventitiously

  D fastidiously

  E punctiliously

  F exiguously

34. To make identifying one animal from another more _____, scientists from different societies have devised various classification systems, but now some scientists are advocating the creation of a single, universal animal classification system for all cultures across the globe to adopt.

  A tamable

  B vociferous

  C resplendent

  D quiescent

  E glib

  F tractable

35. Though both protons and neutrons are housed in the nucleus of an atom, the protons but not the neutrons define the electric charge of the nucleus; neutrons contribute to the mass of the nucleus, but they have no electric charge to _____ to the nucleus.

  A extenuate

  B impart

  C bestow

  D remit

  E bequeath

  F ossify

36.   The nucleus is the most _____ part of an atom; a nucleus's significance lies in that the majority of the atom's mass is located in the nucleus, and, in living organisms, the nucleus is the site where DNA lives and begins to be interpreted by the cell.

   [A]   effulgent

   [B]   substantive

   [C]   epochal

   [D]   indispensable

   [E]   recondite

   [F]   evidentiary

37.   Metabolism is a word that is often _____ with weight loss, but metabolism is associated with many more processes than regulating a person's ability to convert fat to energy; it can refer to all of the chemical reactions that occur inside the cells of living organisms.

   [A]   affiliated

   [B]   colligated

   [C]   caviled

   [D]   distended

   [E]   ensconced

   [F]   abrogated

38.   The exact timing of hurricane season depends on the part of the world under _____, but meteorologists have determined that on average the month of May is the most active month for hurricane activity worldwide while the month of September usually has the least hurricane activity.

   [A]   cogitation

   [B]   consideration

   [C]   circumlocution

   [D]   introspection

   [E]   expatiation

   [F]   rumination

39. Though a significant number of countries are governed as democracies, the government structures that exist around the world are far from _____ ; along with democracies, an assortment of ruling systems including theocracies, technocracies, constitutional monarchies, absolute monarchies, and dictatorships are in use today.

  A bilious

  B lachrymose

  C homogenous

  D undifferentiated

  E discrete

  F disjointed

40. European imperialism redrew the borders of many African nations from the ones that existed before the colonizers arrived; many groups that were _____ before the Europeans' arrival found themselves, as a result of conquest, part of new nations that contained historically unacquainted ethnic groups by the time European rule ended.

  A sequestered

  B parochial

  C insular

  D sectarian

  E illiberal

  F catholic

41. America's founding fathers used compromise to _____ disagreements that arose when assaying the emerging government; for example, the founders determined the best solution would be to create a two-house legislative body in order to suppress conflicts that arose between two factions over how citizens would be represented in the national government.

  A quell

  B castigate

  C emulate

  D exacerbate

  E obviate

  F precipitate

42. The social stigma associated with a conviction for a serious crime can present nearly _____ obstacles for someone attempting to re-enter society and contribute to the citizenry after completing a period of incarceration; a criminal record can prevent a person from finding employment or even voting in certain jurisdictions.

    [A] culpable

    [B] dogmatic

    [C] intransigent

    [D] emollient

    [E] recalcitrant

    [F] florid

43. The components that make up a culture vary depending on the group in question; shared language, experiences, history, food, and language are some of the delineating elements distinguishing one culture from another, but a powerful, albeit intangible, aspect of what defines a culture is an _____ bond members feel for one another.

    [A] irascible

    [B] execrable

    [C] inextirpable

    [D] illustrious

    [E] opprobious

    [F] indelible

44. Media are some of the most effective tools cultural influencers can use to spread their messages to the widest possible audience; some use media to influence others in _____ ways, forwarding fashion and hairstyle trends for example, while others employ media to incite dissension and societal upheaval.

    [A] innocuous

    [B] aberrant

    [C] injurious

    [D] banal

    [E] equivocal

    [F] exorbitant

45.   Extensive liberal arts study was once considered an integral component of a quality education, but as societies have become more technologically, dedicating years to studies in classic literature or philosophy are more often perceived as _____ endeavors that should be set aside for training in more practical study in the sciences or in medicine.

   [A]   erudite

   [B]   lofty

   [C]   asinine

   [D]   obtuse

   [E]   chary

   [F]   fetid

46.   After the fall of the Iron Curtain, multinational corporations acquired companies in countries that had been part of the Soviet Bloc and _____ problems at every level of their new possessions.

   [A]   encountered

   [B]   took on

   [C]   happened upon

   [D]   affronted

   [E]   emulated

   [F]   studied

47.   Although it might not seem apparent to the _____ observer, a watch has more mass when it is wound up than when it is not because when its spring is put into tension, that is, when it is wound up, it experiences an increase in the potential energy it bears and thus it increases in mass.

   [A]   casual

   [B]   concerned

   [C]   curious

   [D]   dispassionate

   [E]   heedless

   [F]   interested

48.   Belief in evolution is based on evidence, otherwise it would be _____.

 [A]   inconceivable

 [B]   implausible

 [C]   questionable

 [D]   incontestable

 [E]   probable

 [F]   cogitable

49.   Males and females can have different management styles, leading sometimes to misunderstandings and when the misunderstandings are not resolved, they can result in decreases in a company's _____.

 [A]   creativity

 [B]   edge

 [C]   effectiveness

 [D]   productivity

 [E]   potency

 [F]   adaptability

50.   Affirmative action programs aimed at increasing the number of women and minorities in upper management can sometimes lead to the white males in the company feeling _____.

 [A]   boorish

 [B]   apprehensive

 [C]   unassertive

 [D]   unfazed

 [E]   uneasy

 [F]   worrisome

51. More so than other types of cells, animal cells are fragile and remain _____ to changes in their immediate environment.

    A   receptive

    B   sensible

    C   sensitive

    D   sensual

    E   sensorial

    F   subject

52. When a company's name becomes synonymous with the product it sells, the company loses its distinctive _____ and other companies can sell similar products as if they were selling the same product as the original company.

    A   ability

    B   advantage

    C   dominance

    D   edge

    E   stranglehold

    F   superiority

53. When workers are invited to use their own individual ingenuity and imagination to solve problems confronting the company, they get a chance to believe that they are _____ to the company and the company is frequently able to become stronger.

    A   fundamental

    B   indispensable

    C   integral

    D   intrinsic

    E   significant

    F   vital

54.   Bruegel's paintings are _____for their vivid colors and realistic representations of peasant scenes such as vomiting and brawling at inns.

   [A]   eye-catching

   [B]   famous

   [C]   glaring

   [D]   notable

   [E]   remarkable

   [F]   tawdry

55.   Except for the _____ example of "The Necklace," Maupassant's short stories are not known for surprise endings, most of his work emphasizes characterization and the exploration of sexuality.

   [A]   famous

   [B]   great

   [C]   ignominious

   [D]   infamous

   [E]   notorious

   [F]   preeminent

56.   The music of the ballet and its composer were _____ in the government-run media and the composer was forced to repudiate his work or risk losing his livelihood.

   [A]   aspersed

   [B]   degraded

   [C]   disgraced

   [D]   exculpated

   [E]   repudiated

   [F]   traduced

57. In response to negative attention in the press following a public performance of his opera, Shostakovich subtitled his next work "An artistic response to just criticism," although many _____ listeners heard sarcasm coming through the seemingly happy moments of the music.

   [A] discriminative

   [B] intensive

   [C] intelligent

   [D] perceptive

   [E] sharp-witted

   [F] veteran

58. Totalitarian governments usually feel threatened by any individual voice that becomes _____ they do what they can to silence such potential problems.

   [A] eminent

   [B] noteworthy

   [C] recognizable

   [D] salient

   [E] significant

   [F] visible

59. Ann Rand wrote that copyrights and patents are a way of _____ a most basic property right, the right to profit from the product of one's own mind.

   [A] effectuating

   [B] legislating

   [C] observing

   [D] promulgating

   [E] protecting

   [F] validating

60.   In his "Letter from Birmingham Jail," Martin Luther King catalogued the multitude of abuses
       experienced by African Americans living in the 1960's in the United States and _____ a course for
       change.

   [A]   calculated

   [B]   drafted

   [C]   framed

   [D]   organized

   [E]   prepared

   [F]   schemed

61.   Martin Luther King's justly famous "Letter from Birmingham Jail," was written in response to a/an
       _____ statement by "Eight Alabama Clergymen" that had been published in newspapers
       throughout the United States.

   [A]   disreputable

   [B]   famous

   [C]   oppugnant

   [D]   opprobrious

   [E]   shoddy

   [F]   vicious

62.   Study after study has _____ that when women and men have similar levels of education and
       similar jobs and work histories ,that men earn more than women and that even when they are children,
       women tend to see themselves earning less money than men when they become adults.

   [A]   manifested

   [B]   projected

   [C]   publicized

   [D]   revealed

   [E]   uncloaked

   [F]   unveiled

63.   When Joseph Stalin attended the premier of Shostakovich's opera "The Nose," he left early, apparently offended by the _____ plot and shocked by the progressive music of the score.

  A   ebullient

  B   gamey

  C   impish

  D   phlegmatic

  E   puckish

  F   ribald

64.   When the Japanese attacked Pearl Harbor on 7 December 1941, their ultimate aim was not to totally defeat the United States, but to win a war of attrition so they could eventually have _____ over the peoples and products of the Eastern Pacific Rim, an outcome the United States would never have accepted.

  A   ascendance

  B   clout

  C   hegemony

  D   privileges

  E   management

  F   reign

65.   As Franz Liszt said, the _____ influence on the musicians of the late 19th century that is, the musicians of the Romantic Period, was the work and towering legacy of Ludwig van Beethoven, the late classical composer who died in 1827.

  A   ancillary

  B   distinguished

  C   notable

  D   preponderant

  E   sovereign

  F   auxiliary

66. At the beginning of the twentieth century, it appeared that Russia was going to become the center of the musical and literary world, but instability in the country and the 1917 October Revolution put an end to any _____ Russia might have enjoyed.

    A clout

    B importance

    C place

    D privilege

    E superintendence

    F sway

67. Charles Dickens is known for the clearly defined characters he creates, his vivid descriptions of settings, and for his efforts to use his work to raise public consciousness about the _____ practices of privileged groups in British society of his time.

    A beneficial

    B benignant

    C co-optive

    D deceptive

    E deleterious

    F exploitive

68. In 2010, an electrician who had worked for Pablo Picasso revealed that he had in his possession a/an _____ of Picasso's work spanning the entire creative career of the artist.

    A argosy

    B collection

    C cornucopia

    D repository

    E stockpile

    F wellspring

69. The Trinidadian author, V. S. Naipaul, won the Nobel Prize for literature in 2001, but is widely
     _____ by Caribbeanists for his allegedly negative portrayals and views of the Caribbean and its
     people.

     [A] chided

     [B] excoriated

     [C] exculpated

     [D] sanctioned

     [E] libeled

     [F] slandered

70. After World War Two, many were _____ by the contrast between the unprecedented
     technological progress of the preceding years and the inability of human societies to get along with
     each other.

     [A] addled

     [B] agitated

     [C] cozened

     [D] deluded

     [E] graveled

     [F] stunned

71. Karl Popper's most important contribution is his statement that if a hypothesis is to have scientific
     _____ it must be testable, that is, there must be a way that can potentially show that the theory is
     wrong.

     [A] condition

     [B] capacity

     [C] position

     [D] rank

     [E] standing

     [F] status

72.   Rather than putting so much _____ in definitions, Karl Popper wrote that it would be better to carefully phrase one's sentences so that the various meanings of the words used would not matter and people would argue less about words.

   [A]   credit

   [B]   dubiety

   [C]   force

   [D]   hope

   [E]   progeny

   [F]   stock

73.   Because the military, economic and social life of any society is _____ by that of other countries, few things take place in any nation that are not related to events in bordering countries.

   [A]   accommodated

   [B]   conditioned

   [C]   habituated

   [D]   inured

   [E]   primed

   [F]   recast

74.   Although in the past biologists kept the subfields of biology separate, in recent years the emphasis has been on the study of the biological phenomena that living things have in common, a search for _____, characteristic of twentieth-century scientific inquiry.

   [A]   universals

   [B]   specifics

   [C]   details

   [D]   circumscription

   [E]   generality

   [F]   precision

75. There is a/an _____ similarity between a 1929 picture of frightened citizens crowding the streets around the New York Stock exchange on the first day of the October Stock Market crash that ushered in the Great Depression and pictures taken seventy-two years later of New Yorkers looking up at the World Trade Center towers on September 11, 2001.

  A eerie

  B curious

  C interesting

  D striking

  E surprising

  F uncanny

76. The facts that all living cells come from pre-existing living cells and all living cells use the same _____ to transmit DNA from one generation to another, pose problems for those who seek to determine the origin of the first living cell.

  A determinant

  B impetus

  C ingredient

  D means

  E mechanism

  F median

77. Although the human body has been studied intensively for centuries, it should not be thought that there is nothing more to learn; scientists will be making _____ discoveries about the body for as long as there are scientists.

  A germinal

  B innovative

  C ingenious

  D novel

  E original

  F primal

78. Two developments that greatly aided advancement in biology in the 17th century were the growth of scientific societies and the further development of the microscope; one aided individual discovery and the other aided _____ among professionals of what had been discovered.

   A dispersal

   B dissipation

   C collection

   D concentration

   E dissemination

   F propagation

79. Although spontaneous generation was debunked in 1688, belief in it persisted for two more centuries until the 1870's, when Louis Pasteur definitively _____ that it could not occur.

   A adduced

   B disconfirmed

   C divulged

   D evinced

   E publicized

   F substantiated

80. Mendel's study of heredity and his imaginative deductions based on the work were completed in the 1860's, but his discoveries did not become widely known until after 1900, largely because an influential botanist of the 1860's failed to see the _____ of Mendel's work and did not lend Mendel his support.

   A preeminence

   B prominence

   C renown

   D significance

   E substantiveness

   F worth

81. _____ dreams of wealth will do you little good as an entrepreneur; research suggests that those with a concrete business plan are twice as likely to succeed as those without.

    A   Nebulous

    B   Sagacious

    C   Craven

    D   Cogent

    E   Dubious

    F   Fervid

82. Edgar Allan Poe's _____ tales of crumbling mansions and dying women are perennial favorites among those with a taste for horror and mystery.

    A   whimsical

    B   morbid

    C   saturnine

    D   sublime

    E   droll

    F   esoteric

83. Ernest Shackleton became famous for his _____ efforts to ensure the survival of his team during the Endurance Expedition; after months of coping with the harsh Antarctic conditions, Shackleton made an 800-mile open-boat voyage in the hopes of seeing his companions rescued.

    A   erudite

    B   dogged

    C   phlegmatic

    D   desultory

    E   preternatural

    F   indefatigable

84. In the musical Camelot, Mordred exposes Lancelot and Guinevere's _____ love affair in his efforts to overthrow King Arthur, Guinevere's husband.

    A inchoate

    B noisome

    C clandestine

    D discrete

    E illicit

    F gauche

85. For scientists concerned about climate change, the recent prevalence of "extreme weather" - hurricanes, droughts, and the like - is an alarming _____ of things to come.

    A portent

    B vagary

    C harbinger

    D antithesis

    E enigma

    F imbroglio

86. Living in groups of up to eighty individuals and engaging in behaviors such as mutual grooming, the chimpanzee is one of nature's most _____ animals.

    A indigenous

    B ascetic

    C peripatetic

    D redoubtable

    E gregarious

    F extroverted

87. When asked where he had been, the suspect _____ spinning an elaborate story but failing to provide any evidence of his whereabouts.

   - [A] fawned
   - [B] equivocated
   - [C] quaffed
   - [D] prevaricated
   - [E] transgressed
   - [F] palpitated

88. Although one-third of the world's population is thought to be infected with tuberculosis, the disease may remain _____ for several years; in many cases, it never becomes active at all.

   - [A] restive
   - [B] inimical
   - [C] latent
   - [D] fulsome
   - [E] quiescent
   - [F] discreet

89. In nineteenth-century Europe, female behavior was subject to the most stringent of social rules; women who _____ convention and had children out of wedlock were often treated as outcasts.

   - [A] wafted
   - [B] extolled
   - [C] flouted
   - [D] spurned
   - [E] disinterred
   - [F] condoned

90.   Although Galileo maintained that his theory of heliocentrism was compatible with Christian belief, Church leaders did not agree, and ultimately brought him before the Inquisition where he was forced to _____ his beliefs.

   A   repudiate

   B   beatify

   C   preclude

   D   foment

   E   accrue

   F   abjure

91.   Although many people assume that research and development tax credits are only available to large companies with money to invest in on-site laboratories and the like, the truth is that even small businesses can be eligible for tax benefits, provided that their work is innovative and their management _____.

   A   shrewd

   B   supine

   C   adroit

   D   dogmatic

   E   ineluctable

   F   meretricious

92.   The mother _____ her child for stealing money from his sister's piggy bank.

   A   placated

   B   castigated

   C   flustered

   D   vilified

   E   upbraided

   F   descried

93. As its name suggests, the "corpse flower" emits a strong and _____ odor that is highly unpleasant to humans.

   - **A**   pusillanimous
   - **B**   effete
   - **C**   fetid
   - **D**   hirsute
   - **E**   noisome
   - **F**   florid

94. Joan of Arc, a peasant girl with no military training and with only her religious convictions to guide her, showed great _____ in asking the Dauphin to entrust her with the French army.

   - **A**   temperance
   - **B**   temerity
   - **C**   mettle
   - **D**   recreancy
   - **E**   paean
   - **F**   fecklessness

95. The relatively _____ weather of northern Europe is in large part due to the Gulf Stream, a warm ocean current originating in the waters off of Florida.

   - **A**   provident
   - **B**   torpid
   - **C**   aseptic
   - **D**   benign
   - **E**   inveterate
   - **F**   propitious

96. The rich and, to some people, strident sound of bagpipes is a far cry from the more _____ tones of so many other instruments.

   A   mellifluous

   B   dulcet

   C   lithe

   D   obstreperous

   E   abstruse

   F   stentorian

97. The fearsome crashing of thunder, which makes so many children _____ and seek their parents, has a surprisingly simple explanation; each bolt of lightning heats the surrounding air, causing it to expand so rapidly that it breaks the sound barrier.

   A   clinch

   B   quail

   C   demur

   D   rebuff

   E   cower

   F   simper

98. Thomas Hobbes, who famously remarked that life in a "state of nature" is "nasty, brutish and short," believed that the _____ of society are all that prevent humanity from succumbing to its basest urges.

   A   cabals

   B   idylls

   C   proscriptions

   D   vacillations

   E   prohibitions

   F   derelictions

99.   Although it seems unlikely that the average person's tastes are as discriminating as those of a _____ it is nevertheless true that 90 percent of restaurants fail within one year of opening.

    [A]   tyro

    [B]   wag

    [C]   virago

    [D]   libertine

    [E]   connoisseur

    [F]   epicure

100.   The audience was unimpressed with the lecture; despite the speaker's dazzling rhetoric and considerable charisma, it was clear that his claims were _____.

    [A]   fervid

    [B]   specious

    [C]   picaresque

    [D]   fallacious

    [E]   officious

    [F]   feckless

101.   To those unfamiliar with Middle Eastern dance, the countless sequins and tassels worn by belly dancers may seem excessive or even _____ however, by accentuating the dancer's movements; such embellishments serve a practical purpose.

    [A]   tawdry

    [B]   piquant

    [C]   voluble

    [D]   raffish

    [E]   aberrant

    [F]   diaphanous

102. Animals that deal with the seasonal shortage of food by hibernating typically _____ themselves beforehand in order to store up enough energy for the winter months.

    [A] incense

    [B] preen

    [C] glut

    [D] recast

    [E] enervate

    [F] gorge

103. Efforts to address the so-called "glass ceiling" have met with only _____ success; although women are twice as likely as men to start up businesses, only 3 percent of these female-owned businesses generate revenue of over $1 million.

    [A] middling

    [B] halcyon

    [C] equivocal

    [D] ecumenical

    [E] sophomoric

    [F] garrulous

104. The teacher was of a _____ disposition, and frequently lashed out at her students over perceived insults.

    [A] stygian

    [B] fatuous

    [C] turbid

    [D] irascible

    [E] splenetic

    [F] recondite

105. Research suggests that those with a _____ for math may have inherited their skills from their parents; a 2009 study revealed that the development of the part of the brain used in calculations is overwhelmingly governed by genetics.

    A   mendacity

    B   aptitude

    C   recidivism

    D   eloquence

    E   dereliction

    F   propensity

106. As anthropologists know, certain practices and beliefs unite the _____ cultures of the world; every known civilization, for example, has practiced some form of religion.

    A   inimitable

    B   profligate

    C   disparate

    D   palatial

    E   myriad

    F   prolix

107. The unique and sometimes visionary premises of independent films are proof of what writers and directors can achieve when not _____ by concerns of money and popularity.

    A   fettered

    B   emaciated

    C   obviated

    D   macerated

    E   satiated

    F   constrained

108. Although the Chinese economy has been growing rapidly for three decades, there is some concern that this expansion will slow as more and more people obtain college degrees; those with a university education will no doubt be _____ to accept the low-paying factory jobs that have contributed to China's success.

[A] crass

[B] nonplused

[C] disinclined

[D] loath

[E] urbane

[F] frantic

109. In order to get the most out of your batteries, keep them at room temperature; cold, for example _____ the chemical reaction that generates power, so the battery must work harder to produce the same amount of power.

[A] retards

[B] vituperates

[C] bedizens

[D] impedes

[E] ameliorates

[F] piques

110. Even during his lifetime, Caligula had a reputation for moral _____; one account had him ordering his guards to throw a group of innocent spectators into the Colosseum's arena to be devoured by wild animals.

[A] desuetude

[B] finesse

[C] probity

[D] degeneracy

[E] insularity

[F] turpitude

111. His _____ disposition was infectious; it was impossible to talk to him and remain unmoved by his enthusiasm.

     [A]   ineffable

     [B]   ebullient

     [C]   blithe

     [D]   lachrymose

     [E]   verdant

     [F]   edacious

112. Terms used in everyday language are not necessarily the most scientifically _____ as the case of the organism known as "seaweed" illustrates; contrary to what its name suggests, seaweed is actually a member of the kingdom Protista.

     [A]   admonitory

     [B]   insouciant

     [C]   felicitous

     [D]   sententious

     [E]   expedient

     [F]   quixotic

113. Given the events that preceded the couple's separation, it is hardly surprising that the divorce proceedings were marked by ill-will and _____.

     [A]   vituperation

     [B]   indolence

     [C]   obloquy

     [D]   vacillation

     [E]   doggerel

     [F]   abeyance

114. Because they can go for several years without erupting, it can be difficult to determine which volcanoes are extinct and which are merely dormant - a _____ state of affairs.

   - [A] disconcerting
   - [B] extenuating
   - [C] trenchant
   - [D] ominous
   - [E] inimitable
   - [F] luculent

115. Given that they account for roughly half of America's GDP, it would be a mistake to _____ the importance of small businesses.

   - [A] broach
   - [B] denigrate
   - [C] glean
   - [D] sanction
   - [E] lionize
   - [F] disparage

116. Faberge eggs are known for the incredibly _____ designs; the first one ever made opened to reveal a gold yolk, which itself concealed a gold hen and a miniature diamond replica of the Russian Imperial Crown.

   - [A] sumptuous
   - [B] ubiquitous
   - [C] ostentatious
   - [D] incipient
   - [E] prudish
   - [F] lugubrious

117. The movement of gas molecules is rather _____; particles move quickly and more or less randomly.

   A   belligerent

   B   turgid

   C   volatile

   D   irrevocable

   E   frenetic

   F   malleable

118. The world's oceans are home to many bizarre and fascinating creatures, but few are more _____ than the octopus, which has three hearts, no bones, and an intelligence level that far exceeds that of other invertebrates.

   A   prosaic

   B   extant

   C   inscrutable

   D   enigmatic

   E   nascent

   F   incredulous

119. The "Trail of Tears" owes its _____ name to the thousands of Cherokees who suffered and often died during their forced relocation westward.

   A   petrous

   B   imperious

   C   pugnacious

   D   evocative

   E   doleful

   F   salubrious

120. It is clear that Mozart, who wrote his first opera at the age of eleven, displayed _____ musical abilities from his earliest years.

   A   prodigious

   B   grandiloquent

   C   preternatural

   D   epicurean

   E   refractory

   F   brazen

This page is intentionally left blank

Chapter 6

Answers and Explanations

Text Completion

1. *Inculcate, potentates* and *iconoclast*

   We can teach logic, but values such as the love or reason and virtue must be instilled. Clearly Socrates did not ingurgitate (A) or gulp his students, or importune (B), meaning inconvenience, them with a love of reasoning and virtue. The love of reasoning and virtue is an abstract quality and something we attempt to inculcate (C) in students, making C the correct answer.

   Those who have authority are not portents (D), as portents are omens or premonitions. They can, however, be referred to as potentates (E) or autocratic rulers. They would not be profligates (F), or recklessly wasteful individuals. Option E is the correct answer.

   Socrates cannot be considered a centurion (G) or leader of a unit of 100 soldiers, but Athenian potents may well have perceived him as an iconoclast (H). Iconoclasts attack or otherwise undermine cherished ideas and institutions including social structures and authorities of the day. Neophyte (I) must be eliminated as neophyte means novice and implies inchoate knowledge and skills; this certainly would not describe a teacher charged with educating the patrician Athenian youth. H is the correct answer.

2. *Sophistry* and *patrician*

   An ingenious yet invalid argument would amount to a dissimulation of the truth, but simple dissimulation, or deceiving, would not lead to the very specific aims Stephens has "to create an ingenious yet invalid argument." Option A, then, can be eliminated. Option B can also be eliminated as it is unlikely Stephens employs hubris or pride to create an ingenious yet invalid argument. Sophistry (C), however, has been employed since the time of the ancient Greek sophists whose specialty was creating ingenious yet invalid arguments aimed at getting readers or listeners to agree with them. Option C, then, is the correct answer.

   If students from the lower socio-economic echelons are penalized, and their peers who don't have to serve can buy their way out of the proposed youth service program, we can safely assume that the latter are affluent youth from socio-economically advantaged families. Erudite (D) can be eliminated as erudite means learned, not socio-economically advantaged. These peers, furthermore, may or may not show off their wealth; the passage does not tell us if they are ostentatious (E). These peers, however, could be described as patrician (F) or deriving from the refined or wealthier class, making F the correct answer.

3.   *confluence*

This sentence is saying that criminologists use both qualitative and quantitative approaches to yield greater insight in their work. They have combined the two approaches. "Reduction" means "decrease." The passage clearly states that criminologists have added to their analysis. "Petulance" means "sullenness." There is no reason to believe that combining qualitative and quantitative measures is "sullen." "Reluctance" means "hesitancy." There is no evidence in the sentence to suggest that the combination of qualitative and quantitative analyses was done hesitantly. "Diaspora" means "migration." This answer makes no sense in the context of the question "Confluence" means "union." The combining of qualitative and quantitative measures can accurately be described as a "union" of measures.

4.   *permeates*

This sentence is saying that rhetoric used to be confined to a field, but now it is not. We want a word to express this idea of rhetoric's newfound ubiquity. "Permits" means "allows." There is no indicationgiven in the passage that rhetoric now "allows" other fields of study to do anything. "Aggrandizes" means "glorifies." Again, the passage is stressing that rhetoric used to be confined, but now it is not. Rhetoric may very well aggrandize every field of study but it is not indicated in the passage. Therefore, it is an incorrect answer. "Aggravates" means "annoys." This answer has the same shortcomings as "Aggrandizes" – it's possible, but there's no specific reference in the passage. "Rectifies" means "fixes." This answer, once again, is given no reference in the passage. We are left with "Permeates." This word means "pervades." This makes sense. If rhetoric used to be confined to political discourse, but is now more widespread, then it would indeed pervade other areas of study.

5.   *perdures*

This sentence is saying that when one thing (written records) fails, another (crude tools) does not. Therefore we want a word to express this enduring quality. "Discontinue" means to "abandon." This is not a word that expresses an enduring quality. "Excavates" means "exhumes." This answer does not make any sense in the context of the question. "Derides" means "scorns." There is no indication given that crude tools "scorn" anything when the written record fails. "Beguiles" means "charms." Again, there is no indication that crude tools "charm" anything when the written record fails. "Perdures" means "continues to exist." This is the exact action that would cause crude tools to "leave a trail throughout time" even when "the written records of events become unclear."

6.   *prejudices*

This sentence is saying how "strict experimentation" introduces something into the human mind, and this "something" makes understanding the results of an experiment more difficult. We want to choose as our answer something that would undermine "strict experimentation." "Pellucidity" means "clarity." Clarity would not undermine strict experimentation. "Impartiality" means "objectivity." Objectivity would not undermine strict experimentation, either. "Riposte" means "comeback." This answer does not make sense in the context of the question. A "Plutocracy" is a type of government, and therefore does not make sense as an answer. "Prejudices" means "biases." The prejudices of the human mind would be able to undermine "strict experimentation."

7.   *attenuate*

This sentence is saying that market competition is good, and then gives an example of the opposite situation. Therefore, the opposite situation (the concentration of market capital in few enterprises) must be bad for the economy. "Consecrate" means "bless." "Blessed" economic health is not a bad thing.

"Commiserate" means "empathize." This answer does not make sense in the context of the question. "Alleviate" means "improve." The sentence clearly implies that concentration of market capital in few enterprises is a bad thing, so it will not improve the economy. "Fulminate" means "criticize." There is no evidence given that the concentration of market capital in relatively few enterprises will criticize the economy. "Attenuate" means "lessen," or "weaken." This is the correct answer. This continues the idea of concentrated market capital being bad for an economy.

8. *obstinacy* and *flouted*

    This passage is stating that the man was too stubborn to listen to his friends' advice about learning guitar. "Pensiveness" means "thoughtfulness." The man would not be amazed by his own thoughtfulness, because he did not act very thoughtful in ignoring his friends' advice. "Reticence" means "reserve." He would not be surprised by his own reserve, either, because he wasn't reserved: he pushed ahead and ignored everyone's advice. We are left with "Obstinacy." This word means "stubbornness." This makes sense. The man would be amazed at his own stubbornness because he ignored all of his friends' advice.

    For the next blank, the passage is stating that the man continued to push his hands hard even though his friends told him to accept a slow progression of skill. "Articulated" means "expressed." The man obviously did not "express" his friends' advice if he continued to push himself hard. "Expounded" means "explained." The man did not explain his friends' advice if he was ignoring it. We are left with "Flouted." This word means "disobeyed." This makes sense. If the man ignores his friends' advice every step of the way then he would be disobeying it.

9. *derided* and *duplicity*

    The passage is stating that Gary often receives criticism for watching television. "Bolstered" means "reinforced." If the people in his life are criticizing television then they are not "reinforcing" it. "Protracted" means "prolonged." Nobody in Gary's life seems to be trying to "prolong" television. "Derided" means "ridiculed." If the people in Gary's life are reprimanding him for watching television, then they are deriding television as a waste of time.

    For the second blank, Gary notices that the same people that deride television often watch it themselves. "Equanimity" means "composure." Gary is not commenting on any sense of composure from the people that deride television, he is criticizing them for deriding television while also watching it. "Sublimity" means "state of high spiritual value." Gary is not commenting on the high spiritual values of these people, he is criticizing them for being dishonest. "Duplicity" means "deceitfulness." If Gary knows that the same people who criticize him for watching television also watch it themselves, he would consider them very deceitful.

10. *exhilarated* and *milquetoast*

    This passage is stating that the idea of riding a motorcycle helps the man break away from his boring existence. "Vetoed" means "prevented." The notion of riding a motorcycle does not prevent the man from doing anything. The passage clearly shows it exciting him and empowering him. "Censured" means "reprimanded." Again, the passage does not show the man being "reprimanded" for wanting to ride a motorcycle. "Exhilarated" means "excited." Riding a motorcycle would cause the man to feel excitement because the rest of his existence is "the safety of an office environment."

    For the second blank, the passage is talking about the type of person the man has always been – very meek. "Obdurate" means "stubborn." Nothing about the description of the man's life describes him as being "stubborn." "Contrarian" means "going against popular opinion." Again, nothing in the passage shows the man contrarian in his life before discovering motorcycles. "Milquetoast" means "meek." One who prefers the "safety of an office environment to anything else" can accurately be described as "milquetoast."

11.   *alleviate* and *begrudge*

This passage is saying that Tiffany has received lots of money, but she knows it will never help her stop missing her parents. "Masticate" means "chew." This obviously makes no sense in the context of the question. "Interpolate" means "include." It doesn't make any sense that Tiffany would want to "include" sorrow in her money. "Alleviate" means "ease." The line "she would rather have had her parents back" shows that money cannot ease Tiffany's pain.

For the second blank, the passage is saying that Tiffany doesn't appreciate the comments that her friends are making. "Lionize" means "idolize." If Tiffany does not like the comments that her friends are making then she would not be idolizing them. "Oblige" means "accommodate." Again, if Tiffany doesn't appreciate her friends' comments then she would not try to accommodate them. "Begrudge" means "resent." If Tiffany didn't appreciate the advice her friends are giving her, then she would "resent" the comments.

12.   *cliche* and *appalling*

The passage is stating that Howard feels like his experience is unique, even though he apparently knows that it is not. "Facetious" means "foolish." Howard does not seem to find his story foolish, because it is causing him much consternation. "Metaphorical" means "symbolic." This situation is really happening to Howard, so it is not symbolic. "Cliche" means "overused." This answer works. The first sentence implies that even though Howard feels like his situation is new, it might not be. "Cliche" opposes the word "new," so this is the correct answer.

For the second blank, the passage is talking about all of the bad side effects Howard will face after signing his record contract. "Inconsequential" means "unimportant." If what Howard was doing to the prices that his fans pay was "unimportant" then it would not be giving him so much pause. "Judicious" means "sensible." If Howard was charging sensible prices to his fans then he would not be so concerned. "Appalling" means "dreadful." Howard would feel bad if the prices he was charging to his "loyal fans" were "dreadful."

13.   *elucidation* and *generalities*

From the passage, readers can tell that the predictions made by horoscopes are generic and manipulable and their comprehension, explication and application can be easily changed to fit almost any situation. We are looking for a synonym for "understanding" or "interpretation" to complete the first blank. Palpability (A) means touchable and implies a sense of reality that is not present in generic horoscopes. Elucidation (B), meaning explanation or explication, however, fits and is the correct answer. If we can explain something, we understand it. Option C can be eliminated as omnipotence refers to the quality of being all powerful and does not fit in the context of this sentence. Option B is the correct answer.

Horoscopes are better applied to the general aspects than to the specific details of our lives. Clearly, we are looking for the correct synonym for "generic details "to complete Blank (ii). Exigencies, or extreme moments that demand attention, vary from person to person and are not the domain of horoscopes. They tend to be anything but generic, so Option D, then, can be eliminated. We must distinguish between shades of meaning to choose between options E and F. Generalizations (E) are generalities that are stated audibly or in print, and E must consequently be eliminated. The passage, however, refers to the generalities (F), or general/generic aspects of our lives, making F the correct answer.

14.   *endemic* and *congruous*

An endemic disease is one that is constantly present, as in "malnutrition is endemic to certain impoverished regions of Africa." Option A, then, does not actually describe the world-wide flu of 1918 and must be eliminated. An epidemic (C) is a widespread outbreak of infectious disease making epidemic (C) a strong contender for correct answer. However, before selecting C, we must consider option B, pandemic. A pandemic is an epidemic that occurs throughout a large region or, as in the passage above, throughout the entire world. Clearly, option B, is the word that actually describes the flu that ravaged the entire world in 1918 and the correct answer.

The fact that world leaders came together to develop a single strategy for dealing with mass infections suggests that said strategy is comprehensive and homogenous. Option D, congruous, means harmonious/homogenous and reflects the homogeneity of a single worldwide strategy for addressing pandemics. Option E, germane means relevant or appropriate, and does not reflect the singleness of purpose of a single worldwide approach. Option F, refractory, meaning difficult to manage does not fit the context of the sentence and must be eliminated, making D, congruous, the correct answer.

15. *acumen*

Although the scientists may have all carried themselves in the same way, thus affecting a "combined demeanor" such a demeanor (A) would have no bearing on the scientists' predictions and makes little sense in the context of the sentence. The sentence, furthermore, gives us no reason to suspect the scientists of heresy (B). Even if they were all heretics, their heresy would have no bearing on their predictions or the events that followed the launch. Option C can be eliminated because it takes knowledge and critical thinking, not efficacy or efficiency, to predict events. The combined acumen (D), or expertise, of the scientists, however, should have enabled them to foresee problems and predict what came to pass, making D the correct answer. The callousness (E) of the scientists is not relevant to the remainder of the sentence. As we do not rely on callousness, but acumen, to make predictions, E must also be eliminated. Option D is the correct answer.

16. *refulgent*

The lifestyles described here are clearly ostentatious, though that is not one of the options. We must look, then, for a synonym for ostentatious. Refulgent (A), meaning gleaming or radiant is a good match for ostentatious as both denote notable radiance or opulence. Austere (B), on the other hand, means severe, somber, self-disciplined and is clearly the antithesis of the word needed here. Laudable (C) can hardly apply as the passage makes clear that the lives depicted are not laudable or praiseworthy. Monotonous (D) must be eliminated because there is no indication that the stars' lifestyles are repetitive and boring. Option E must be eliminated as the passage does not support the idea that the stars' lives are sanctimonious or hypocritically pious. Option A, refulgent, is the correct answer.

17. *harangue*

Here we are looking for a word that describes the loud and adamant denial the defendant is making. Option A can be eliminated as dyspepsia means indigestion and has no application here. Option B, harangue, on the other hand, means a loud or bombastic declamation and makes sense in the context of the sentence. Option C, approbation, meaning praise can also be eliminated as it makes no sense in the context of the sentence. Peregrination, option D, can be eliminated as a period of wandering or travels, does not make sense here. Finally, option E, gaucherie, must be eliminated as the defendant's denial is not a case of tactless and socially awkward behavior but a harangue. Option B is the correct answer.

18. *travesty*

We can use tone and syntax to arrive at the right answer to this question. Words like "heinous industry" and "depraved owners" tell us that the author adamantly disapproves of dog fighting and those who fight dogs. Furthermore the sentence structure and particularly the word "of" that occurs after the blank require that we find a word that works within this structure. A tirade (D) is a prolonged period of bitter denunciation or criticism and does not make sense within the sentence. Furthermore, we would not say a "tirade of justice." Artifice (B), meaning a hoax, can be eliminated as can debauch, meaning to corrupt through sensual pleasures (C); they do not make sense in the context of the sentence. Travesty (D), when used with the word "of" as in "a travesty of justice" means a debased imitation. Option D makes sense and is consistent with the syntax of the sentence. Certainly the author of this passage would agree that dog fighting is a debased imitation of a sport. Apparition (E) must be eliminated as apparition means ghost, and would make little sense here. Dog fighting is not a ghost of sport but a travesty of sport, making option D the correct answer.

19.   *prolix*

Any play that is eight hours long and takes two nights to be executed is bound to be tedious. It cannot be pedantic, as this is a word reserved for people who are ostentatious about their leaning. And though the play might well be odious (B) odious simply means hateful and does not reflect the excessive length of the play. Onerous (C), meaning difficult, can also be eliminated as onerous means difficult but does not speak to the length of the play, and moribund (D), meaning being on the point of death could describe play-goers but cannot describe a play that can close but cannot literally die. Prolix (F) means excessively long and tedious and this word effectively describes the world most tedious play. Option F is the correct answer.

20.   *butte*, *capitulated* and *detritus*

The speaker cannot be watching his town wash away from an estuary (A) or river, or he would have washed away as well. Neither can he be watching from a ravine (B), as being in a narrow steep-walled canyon would not place him above the town or afford him a vista. He could, however, watch the town below being swept away from a butte (C) or hill rising abruptly from the surrounding, flat landscape.

The barriers did not countenance (E), meaning placate or pacify as this would make no sense in the context of the sentence. Neither did they assuage (F) or soothe the flood waters. The makeshift barriers obviously gave in or capitulated (D) to the rising flood waters.

Neither calumny (G) nor aspersion (H) make sense in the context of the sentence. Both refer to verbal attacks meant to destroy reputations or friendships (calumny) or disparaging remarks (aspersions) that cast doubt. Aspersion, furthermore, is almost invariably used in the plural with the word "cast" as in "*cast aspersions*." The town washed away like so much debris or detritus (J), for it is indeed the detritus that gets sucked down the drain.

21.   *palliative*

The words "care," "aging" and the phrase "over the long run" are the keys to answering this question. As there is no cure for aging, the focus here is very clearly on providing long-term care aimed at assuaging the pain and discomforts of the geriatric patients referred to rather than care aimed at achieving a cure. Ameliorative (A) care, however, would be any care that meliorates or makes better. That could include improving to the point of recovery, in which case we would no longer be talking about the long-term care that is the focus of this sentence. Palliative (B) care is provided to people when there is no hope for cure, the aim being to alleviate their suffering or symptoms as they degrade. It is the kind of care that nursing homes traditionally provide elderly clients, making patients comfortable until they "pass." Exogenous (C) must be eliminated as it means "deriving from "without;" it sounds good, but is irrelevant to the sentence. Salubrious (D), meaning healthy, must be eliminated as it does not make sense in the context of the sentence. Proprietary (F), pertaining to property or proprietorship must also be eliminated as it does not logically complete the sentence or have a match. Palliative care is long-term alleviative care making option B the correct answer.

22.   *scions*

The list of Henry's children's names following the blank in the second sentence strongly suggests that we are looking for a word that means the equivalent of offspring. We are not looking for the word "heir" from sentence 1, as there can only be one heir to the throne. Progenitors (A), means ancestors, not offspring and must consequently be eliminated. Scions, however, not only means offspring, it means elite or royal offspring from noble or noteworthy families. Clearly option B fits in the context of the sentence. Devisees (C), on the other hand, may include offspring, but may also refer to anyone to whom property is devised by means of a will, related or not." Lineage (D) is related to ancestry, but refers specifically to one's line of descent back from, not forward to, from a common ancestor. Promulgations (F) refer to bulletins or announcements, not offspring and must be eliminated. Henry's offspring would be scions (B).

23. *innocuous, surreptitiously* and *ubiquitous*

The word "although" is critical to this sentence, suggesting that the name belies the true nature of the Kiss-Kiss beetle. The passage tells us the Kiss-Kiss beetle is a dangerous and prevalent pest vector of Chagras Disease. If its name suggests it is the opposite of its true nature, we can assume that its name suggests it is innocuous, option A. The name is suggestive but not foreboding or portentous (B), and the name is not accumbent (C), or reclined, as this would make little sense in the passage. The name of the Kiss-Kiss beetle hides its true nature suggesting it is innocuous (A).

Based on the description of how the Kiss-Kiss beetle enters homes, including words like "infiltrates" and "ensconce" we can safely infer that the bug enters homes surreptitiously (D). Precipitously (E), or abruptly, does not account for the secretive qualities of the beetle and must consequently be eliminated as an option. Finally, quintessentially can be eliminated as it means representing the ultimate or perfect example, leaving us to wonder, "example of what?" As the Kiss-Kiss beetle enters furtively and hides itself, surreptitiously (D) is the correct answer.

The phrase, "Once thought to be rare" that opens the second sentence suggests that it is now known that the Kiss-Kiss beetle is the opposite of rare, or highly prevalent. We must consequently look for a synonym for "highly prevalent." Ubiquitous (G) means everywhere, and if the beetle is highly prevalent it is everywhere. Option G, then, is the correct answer. The beetle is not exiguous (H), meaning scanty, nor is it anomalous, meaning atypical. The Kiss-Kiss beetle is what it is, and what it is, in this instance, is ubiquitous (G).

24. *Recidivism*

When faced with a passage without a topic, focus on what, specifically the passage is about. In this case, the passage is about prisoners, but more specifically, it is about ex-offenders and reoffending. The passage does not deal with the topic of gasconade (A) as this refers to sessions or incidents of extravagant boasting, and gasconade has no relevance to the passage. The passage does, however, address the matter of recidivism (B), or in simple terms, reoffending. It does not deal with exfiltration (C), or clandestine rescues, or with chicanery (D), trickery and deception. Attenuation (E) must also be eliminated as the passage is not about weakening or reducing but about recidivism.

25. *Inveigh* and *rapturous*

To suborn (A) involves secretly deceiving someone and, very significantly, includes tricking that person into committing a crime. Although Felix is clearly tricking his mother and her lover, there is no indication he is inducing them to commit a crime, and option A must consequently be eliminated. Cajole (B), meaning to persuade by means of flattery or promises, does not relate as Felix does not make use of either. Felix inveighs (C), meaning that he entices and manipulates his mother and her lover into believing in a complete fabrication, making option C correct.

If Felix refers to himself as "beyond beatific," or beyond blissful, we can safely say he was rapturous (E). Felix cannot be described as desultory (D) as this means unfocused or jumpy, and Felix is clearly focused on his performance and the pleasure he derives from it. Option D must be eliminated. Felix's behavior is certainly a departure from the normal or right path, psychologically speaking, but he does not feel and would not describe how he felt as aberrant (F). He feels absolutely rapturous as stated in option E

26. *peccadilloes* and *cant*

As adumbrations are faint images, real or metaphorical, option A does not really fit in the context of this sentence. Option B refers to lovers or patrons of the arts and does not fit into the existing structure of the sentence either and so must be eliminated. Peccadilloes (C) or minor infractions on the slightly depraved side, would, however, give parishioners good reason to let the pastor's comments on their shortcomings go in one ear and out the other without going so far as to galvanizing them to leave the church.

Chit-chat (D) refers to idle conversation among a few individuals, but here we have a pastor addressing his congregation, regaling rather than chatting with them. There is no indication from the passage that the pastor is guilty of invective or rough or crude speech, so option E must be eliminated. Invective (E) would not, at any rate, fit grammatically within the existing sentence. Cant (F), or overstated and somewhat hypocritical statements supporting morality and piety does fit the context of the passage and

is the correct answer.

27. *Reconnaissance, glitches* and *go back to the drawing board*

In all probability the SR7 Rover, designed to go out into space and gather intelligence, would not be named a Canard (A) Rover as canard means a derogatory story, report or rumor. Option A certainly does not imply the exploratory nature of the mission but rather raises questions about its legitimacy. Neither would the Rover be named Alliance (C) as that would imply a pact between organizations or nations that is not supported by the passage. The SR7 is going out on a reconnaissance (B) mission to conduct an on-the-ground search/investigation with the aim of bringing back information for the superiors, in this case, the scientists.

Clearly the SR7 suffers from a number of small problems or glitches (F) that are not significant on their own, but when taken together have the potential to delay the launch of the Rover. If the project were merely riddled (loaded) with gimmicks (D), or ingenious and novel stratagems to attract attention and increase appeal, there probably would be no threat to the launch. Furthermore, gimcracks (E) being showy, insignificant trifles such as one might pick up at a country fair, are not the issue here, and option E must be eliminated. F, glitches, or small, or idiosyncratic problems, is the correct answer.

Taking the bull by the horns is synonymous with taking action, and taking action, in this case amounts to launching the SR7. Option H must be eliminated as it would make the sentence repetitive and nonsensical, suggesting that scientists "...launch the SR7 or launch the SR7." Scientists should not throw the baby out with the bathwater (I), or scrap the entire SR7 because of a few glitches, but should "launch the SR7 or go back to the drawing board" to redesign it as stated in option J.

28. *ameliorated*

Clearly Aristotle damaged the reputation of octopi by calling them stupid, and clearly their reputation has been restored by the clever antics of Andy the octopus. With that in mind, we can eliminate option A, as their reputation has not been ruminated, meaning chewed or pondered, by Andy. Their reputation can be described as bifurcated, or divided into two branches (stupid and brilliant in this case) but note that it was not Andy who bifurcated it. Andy has not expedited (C), or sped up the reputation of octopi, but has ameliorated (D), or improved their reputations. Option E can be eliminated as Andy has not scintillated or caused the reputation of octopi to glow or burst forth in flames. Scintillated, furthermore, has no match among the options given. Andy has ameliorated or improved the reputation of octopi, making D the correct answer.

29.   *produce, acreage* and *fruitage*

    Calumny is a misrepresentation or slander, *produce* (as a noun) is a product, usually agricultural, and a *morass* is a marsh or a confusing and difficult situation. Since the text is discussing growing vegetables, the only possible answer for Blank (i) is *produce*.

    For the second blank, *acreage* means an amount of land, a *nadir* is the lowest point, and a *quagmire* is a situation that is difficult to extract oneself from. In the context of planning your garden, only *acreage* makes logical sense.

    The last blank needs a word that means the vegetables that have grown. *Concurrence* is a convergence or simultaneous occurrence; *fruitage* is the harvest or yield, usually from an agricultural endeavor, and *exculpation* an acquittal. Again the correct answer should be obvious – *fruitage* is the only word that fits.

30.   *Cyber, vulnerability* and *puissance*

    After reading the entire text, it should be easy to tell that the answer for Blank (i) is A. The passage is talking about hackers and computer programmers and *cyber* criminals work online and with technology.

    The Nasdaq is an American stock exchange and it was hacked, so the second blank must mean

    something similar to being open to an attack by hackers. *Vulnerability* (how capable something is of being attacked or how susceptible it is to danger) means exactly that.

    Puissance means force or strength, and thus makes it the best choice for the third blank, rather than *nostrum* (a panacea or a sham cure) or *cynosure* (a thing that attracts notice because of its beauty or brilliance).

31.   *precipitous, competitors* and *consistently*

    The options for the first blank are *propitious* (favorable or auspicious), *precipitous* (steep), or *promontory* (an outcropping or peninsula). We can immediately cross off *promontory* as it does not fit logically or grammatically. A drop in profits is rarely a positive thing, and 19 percent is rather high, so the only reasonable choice is B.

    The second blank could be filled with a variety of words. However an *assailant* is an attacker, and *hindrances* is vague, so the best and most logical choice is *competitors* – in Asia it makes sense for these other countries to have companies competing for the same business.

    The last sentence logically must be making the point that GM will be in trouble if it does not perform better. *Erratically,* or unstable and unpredictable, is not a positive thing when talking about a business's performance, and *pedantically,* didactically and pompously, does not make sense in this context either. Performing *consistently,* steadily or evenly, is a positive thing that GM would want to do.

32.   *accentuate , apperception* and *perpetuating*

    The text is about the attempt to both embrace modernizing reforms and maintain a Tatar identity, so the first blank must be *accentuate* (give importance to or stress), rather than *desiccate* (to dry out or dehydrate) or *abrogate* (to revoke or annul).

    If the Tatars are developing a secular approach, then they must finding a new *apperception,* or understanding, of Islam.

    Since the entire passage has been about how Tatars continued to maintain, or perpetuated, their identity, H is the only reasonable choice for the third blank.

33.   *components, tangible* and *alleviates*

    The first blank is part of a comparison. The second half – dealing with each question one at a time –

tells us that the first half must mean the opposite of that, or dealing with all the parts at once. *Components* means pieces or parts, and therefore is the only acceptable choice.

The second blank is also a comparison. *Ephemeral* and *amorphous* mean not concrete or lacking form, while *tangible* means the opposite. In this comparison concrete action is the more logical opposition to continued negotiations, so *tangible* is the best choice.

Both *alleviate* and *exterminate* could work logically in the last sentence – the phased approach could lessen (*alleviate*) or destroy/get rid of (*exterminate*) the immediate pressures. However, grammatically and stylistically only *alleviate* fits.

34.   *demographics, sympathetic* and *dispossessed*

The first blank can only be filled in after reading the entire passage, which is about migration of ethnic groups. Thus we know that the first blank is about the changing ethnic make-up of Abkhazia, or its *demographics*.

If the Abkhazians were leaving after revolts against the Russians failed, then they probably were also somewhat anti-Russian, or at least were *sympathetic* to (agreed with, looked on with favor) anti-Russian activity.

For the last blank, we know that the groups, or peoples, were moved from their homes – they were expelled, kicked out, which is what *dispossessed* means. The phrase "ethnic cleansing" makes it doubtful that they were mollified and content (*appeased*) or self-assured and pleased (*complacent*).

35.   *ecologists, monogamous* and *biodiversity*

This text is about plants and animals and their relationship, and *ecologists* study the interaction between organisms and their environment. There is nothing in the passage relating to codes and ciphers (what *cryptologists* study) or rocks and the composition of the earth (what *geologists* study).

The bees stay with a single flower, so the second blank needs to describe a relationship where you are with only one person – *monogamous*, not *polygamous* (a relationship between several people) or *hypergamous* (a relationship with someone of higher status or more wealth).

The passage claims that it is important for an ecosystem to have a larger number of species (in this case bee species), or *biodiversity*. Neither *anathemas* (despised or repugnant things) nor *surfeit* (an overabundance) make sense in this context.

36.   *an expedient, presumptively* and *implications*

Expedient (suitable or advantageous) is the only valid choice for the first blank given that the method is also described as simple and useful. There is no reason to think that it is a bad idea (*imprudent*) or that it was unnecessary (*superfluous*).

For the second blank the best choice is E – since the scientists are hopeful for the future of the enzyme it can hardly be *dubious* (unlikely) that it will be used to cure diseases. Since the scientists are "not yet sure" how exactly it will be used, *presumptively* (in all likelihood, presumably) is the best fit.

Curing diseases and reprogramming cells is a concrete, not an *abstract* use of the enzyme. The last blank has to be a word that is similar to possibilities or repercussions: *implications*.

37.   *physics ,interference* and *observed*

Gravity and surface tension refer to laws of *physics*, not *biology* or *geology*.

Being able to slide through a tiny hole or climb **up** the side of a glass implies that these laws are not in effect, or are not *interfering* with the movement of the superfluid.

And while *envisioned* could possibly work for the final blank, *observed* is much more appropriate, especially considering that scientists rarely make assumptions without experimenting and observing to check their validity.

38.   *an escalation*, *smaller-grained* and *an accelerated and expensive*

That the erosion (wearing away of rocks and other deposits on the earth's surface) is substantial is clear from the phrase "large amounts of lost sediment." To *escalate* means to intensify or accelerate, and thus A is the correct answer.

D, E, and F could all be possibilities for Blank (ii), but the only option that would plausibly result in faster erosion is *smaller-grained*.

The final blank requires some inference. Given the information we have that beach nourishment causes fast erosion, *accelerated* and *never-ending* are appropriate descriptions of the cycle of erosion and replacement. *Ineffective* is possible, but not as good a fit as the other two options. We understand the process, so it is not *inexplicable*, and we are given no reason to believe it is *unhygienic*. It is safe to assume that having to replace the sand again and again is *expensive*, so G is the best choice.

39.   *immutable*

Immutable means unchanging, and unchangeable. The size of an object is not changed and cannot be changed by distance from the viewer. Option A is the correct answer. Flexible is an antonym and suggests that the size of an object can and will change depending on the distance from the viewer. Stable suggests that object size *is* changeable, but remains temporary unchanged. Abiding suggests that the object remains unchanged because it adheres to a rule, rather than because it is of a constant size. Abiding, like stable includes the possibility of change in size. Uniform suggests that all objects are the same size.

40.   *interpretation*

To interpret is to bring out the meaning of information or stimuli. Option B is the best choice for the blank. Insight is knowledge of the true nature of stimuli, usually through intuitive understanding, and does not apply. Translation changes information to fit new requirements. To elucidate is to explain something that is complicated. To adapt is to change for a new application. In this case, the sentence describes the process of receiving stimuli, then deriving or bringing out meaning by sorting through the available information.

41.   *ascertains*

To ascertain is to find out definitely. If one assumes or theorizes, he or she guesses based on varying evidence. Since this passage refers to learning, ascertain is applicable making option C the best choice. To validate is to confirm what is already known. This passage describes the process of learning through repeated experiences, rather than validating prior knowledge. Disputes is an antonym for assumes and doesn't make sense in the sentence, because if one disputed which route was shorter, he or should would not like to adopt that route.

42.   *unheeded*

To note information is to consciously acknowledge it is present. Information that is unheeded is noted, but not considered. Choice A is the best choice. Information that is rejected may not be noted. Considered is a synonym for "deserve focus" and does not fulfill the contrast suggested by the sentence. Abandoned suggests the information is considered, but later given up; this would suggest the information deserved and received focus, which again does not fit the contrast established in the sentence. Underestimated suggests the information is more important than the subject is aware of and doesn't make sense with the definition of signal detection.

43. *appreciable*

Appreciable stimuli are easily noticed. Negligible and imperceptible stimuli are not easily noticed. Pronounced and significant stimuli are substantially present, which means they may dominate an environment. The sentence does not indicate that the stimuli are strong and the examples indicate subtle stimuli making option E the best choice.

44. *Propel,* *constricts* and *depleted*

To propel is to cause something to move forward. The contraction of the heart muscle moves blood forward and out of the muscle. To pitch is to throw, which does not apply to liquid moved through a closed system. Influence and project should be eliminated. Project is similar to pitch as it refers to throwing or casting something out. The sense of force and forward motion is not evident.

To constrict is to squeeze from all sides. To compress is to press together to create a solid mass. To cinch is to circle something with a tight grip. Constricts is the correct choice as it refers to the pressure exerted to send blood out of the heart.

Depleted means seriously decreased or exhausted. Blood depleted of oxygen must be enriched. Squandered means wasted. The oxygen in the blood is not wasted; rather it is consumed by the body systems. Augmented is an antonym, which means added to. As the blood travels the circulatory system different organs and systems use the oxygen. By the time the blood returns to the heart, the oxygen has been depleted making it the best choice.

45. *procure* and *rudimentary*

To annex is to attach, usually to something larger or more important. To procure is to obtain by some special means. To relinquish is to give up. Since the cells obtain nutrients, and release waste, the word procure is most accurate. If a cell were to annex nutrients, those nutrients would remain attached to the cell surface, rather than incorporated. Thus, procure is the most appropriate choice.

A rudimentary animal is simple with a very basic structure. Primitive suggests a lack of complete development, which does not apply since the sponge is completely developed; it is not a damaged or mutated creature. Vestigial, like primitive indicates the animal is left from another time. Vestigial, however, does not describe the complexity of the organism. A vestigial organism could be quite complex.

46. *impairment* and *pervasive*

Since diabetes leads to blindness, it is logical that it impairs vision. Impaired vision may result in diminished sight, but the words are not synonymous. Impaired means damaged, while diminished means only lessened or decreased. Stagnation is the slowing or stopping of an action, which does not apply.

Pervasive means widespread and has a negative connotation. Pervasive conditions are serious and difficult to control. So, pervasive is the correct answer. Circumscribed means controlled or contained. Capacious means roomy or capable of holding a great quantity and is not applicable.

47. *cadre* and *secrete*

A cadre is a group that works together on similar goals. The different glands in the endocrine system are a cadre as each gland releases a different hormone. A force is a group charged with a specific mission. It is clear that there are multiple "missions" of the endocrine system both inside and outside of the body. The crux is the pivotal point. The endocrine system is made up of glands; it is not a unique entity.

The reader will likely make a determination between disperse and secrete. To disperse is to scatter.

Since the hormones go directly into the blood stream, there is no scattering. The process of secretion is that of releasing a hormone into a system, in this case the circulatory system. Beget refers to giving birth or producing. Again, this sentence refers to the function of releasing the hormones, not creating or producing them.

48. *osmose* and *deliquesce*

The contrast for this word is between the action of the single-celled organisms that obtain nutrients directly, and the more complex organisms that have structures for obtaining and breaking down food sources. To osmose is acquire gradually and unconsciously, without effort. This concept directly contrasts the processes of multi-celled organisms. Thus option A is the best choice for the blank.

Exude refers to output, not intake, and is not applicable. Cull is to select or choose. While the passage indicates that multi-cell organisms may select food sources, that point is not made about single-celled organisms. To extract nutrients multi-cell organisms dissolve or melt the food source. Deliquesce means to melt or dissolve. Flux is a general term for melting, but doesn't apply to liquefying elements. Coagulate is an antonym meaning to join elements of a liquid into a solid or semi-liquid.

49. *heritable*

Gene theory studies which traits are transmitted genetically. Since this passage mentions traits and genetics, one can assume Mendel studied traits that are transmitted to different generations. Bequeathed suggests a conscious action and selectivity, which is not accurate. Inbred does not apply as it refers to the process of breeding, not the resultant genetics. Maternal describes one line of genetic transfer. Acquired traits are those not heritable. Heritable is therefore the answer, as it refers to traits transmitted genetically.

50. *extant*

Extant cells are cells that already exist. The distinction between new cells deriving from extant cells and those cells simply appearing is the main point of this sentence. This sentence clearly makes the comparison. The required word must be a contrast to the idea of cells that "spontaneously appear." Inanimate cells are non-moving cells; it is not clear if these cells exist or spontaneously appear. Neither living, surviving, or mortal, describing the life-state of cells makes a specific contrast to "spontaneously appear."

51. *foundation*

Hooke's work was the basis for future theory, therefore, foundation is correct. Infrastructure is not accurate, as he did not build all the necessary components for future study. Hooke's theory was innovative in that it was new, but innovative does not include the notion that Hooke created a starting point for other scientists. Consequence suggests a cause and effect relationship. If one were to replace the blank with effect, the sentence would not make sense. Production refers to something that is created or produced. Hooke himself did not produce the cell theories that were to follow his discovery.

52. synergy

Synergy means cooperation or collaboration. The cells clearly do not simply co-exist. They work together for the functions to occur. There is nothing in the sentence to suggest agreement or communion. The cells could reasonably have conflicting functions necessary for processes to occur. Accord and intimacy also suggest relationships between the cells other than cooperation. Contention is an antonym and should be eliminated.

53. *cooperatives*

The important detail is that the individual cells in the group are specialized and that they work together. A cooperative is an organization of entities that works together for the benefit of all involved. An organism's functions would obviously benefit all of the component cells; thus, A is the answer. An aggregate is a collection of different units into a single body. This is not a completely inaccurate choice, but is not as precise as it does not indicate the cooperative nature of the body. A collective is similar to an aggregate, and, again, the concept of cooperation or benefiting the whole through group effort is not indicated. A division is a part of the whole. Unanimity refers to the state of being in agreement. Since the cooperative cells perform different functions, they are not in agreement.

54.   orbits and analogous

The context of this sentence makes clear analogy. The behavior of electrons around the nucleus is a planetary model. That is, electrons orbit the nucleus as the planets orbit the sun in the solar system. To orbit is to revolve around another body in a specific path. To envelop is to cover completely. The electrons do not cover the nucleus. To converge is to move toward a single point. This passage describes the path of a rotation around a point, not a movement toward that point.

Since the comparison looks at similarities, the correct choice is analogous. Components which are analogous show likenesses or similarities. Components which are homologous are identical and are derived from shared sources. This term is generally applied to biological elements. Retrogression refers to a return to a prior development stage. There is no mention of evolution or development in this passage.

55.   *unalloyed* and *multifarious*

An alloy is a metal created by combining two or more pure metallic elements. Elements, by definition, are pure. The metal is not alloyed, or combined with other metals or other elements. Elements are, therefore, unalloyed. Something that is adulterated is impure. As noted, an element is pure in that it is made of a single component and is not alloyed or combined with other components. Veritable is similar to literal and is used to indicate that something named is true, realistic, and not imaginary.

Multifarious describes something that occurs with great variety. A multifarious grouping of elements would include those with few, if any, common characteristics. In another context, a multifarious library might include books on tax law, religious tomes from different sources, and children's rhyming books about bears. Something that is homogenous is made up of many components that share some similarity. A homogenous library might contain mystery novels by different authors. Conglomerate describes a mass made of different, varied sources which remain whole, rather than blend together.

56.   *Inverse* and *familiar*

Conforming can be eliminated from the choices, as it refers to actions that are similar and this passage describes actions that are dissimilar. The connection is an almost exact opposite; as one variable increases, the other decreases. Contradictory is similar in meaning, but not a direct opposite. The correct answer is inverse, meaning opposite.

Proverbial should be eliminated as the context does not apply. Mundane can mean dull, which is not supported with context. The word, obvious, after the blank indicates that the example is quite known or familiar. The correct response, therefore, is familiar.

57.   *conjunctly*

This sentence is saying that even though we have two different types of law (criminal and civil) they both still maintain social order. Therefore, we can infer that they work as a team. "Perniciously" means "wickedly." There is no evidence given in this passage that civil and criminal law work "wickedly." The only implication is that they most likely work together. "Superciliously" means "condescendingly." Again, there is no implication that civil and criminal laws combine to function condescendingly. "Redundantly" means "superfluously." The sentence clearly describes the two as having separate purposes (with criminal laws having greater consequences), so they cannot be described as redundant. "Intractably" means "stubbornly." Again, there is no implication given that the two work "stubbornly" together. "Conjunctly" means "cooperatively." This makes sense. Since civil and criminal laws function in different ways, they would have to work conjunctly in order to maintain social order.

58.   *encumbrance* and *reticent*

The passage is stating how the field of meteorology has been pulled, against its will, into the world of politics. This is described as being a burden on meteorologists. Note that the first blank is difficult to answer without reading the rest of the passage. Working in the context of political discourse is not inherently good or bad, so further reading is necessary to establish what answer to choose. After reading, however, it becomes clear that political discourse is undesirable for meteorologists. "Auspices" means backing, or support. Given what we learn about the relationship between political discourse and meteorology, this word doesn't fit. "Insight" means "intuition." Once again, this word does not describe how political discourse effects meteorology "Encumbrance" means "burden," or "hindrance." Given what we learn in the passage, political discourse would be a burden to the study of meteorology.

The second blank describes scientists being thrust into another world. Given the use of the word "thrust," we can infer they were forced to be there. Therefore, we want words that establish the personality of a person who does not want to be in a public situation. "Ostentatious" means "flashy." A person like this would want to be in public situations. "Conspiratorial" is a word that means of or relating to unsavory and secretive behavior. There's no evidence provided in the passage that suggest that meteorologists would want to partake in unsavory and secretive behavior. "Reticent" means "quiet," or "discreet." It makes sense that a quiet person would only enter a public forum when being "thrust" into it.

59.   *antagonistic* and *inscience*

The passage is trying to establish the difficulties that arise in trying to promote new ideas in the world of academia. The first blank is talking about something happening to potential growth in the field of physics. Since this thing is happening "in spite of immense intellect," we can infer that it must be negative. "Correlated" means connected. This word doesn't describe growth being inhibited or promoted, so it doesn't work. "Supplanted" means replaced. This answer does not make sense in the context of the question. We are left with "Antagonistic," which means "opposed to," or "hostile." Having factors that are "opposed" to growth makes sense.

The second blank is the end of a list that states the obstacles a progressive person would face. We want a word that completes this list. "Eminence" means renown. This doesn't continue the tone of the list. "Acquiescence" means compliance. This is of course the opposite of what we want. "Inscience" means "ignorance." Ignorance would function like "entrenched logic" and "petty careerism" in inhibiting society from accepting new ideas.

60.   *enraptured , abstruse* and *charlatans*

The passage states that Fiona is very interested in dreams and what they reveal about the dreamer. "Vindicated" means "justified." The passage doesn't state that Fiona in any way feels "justified" by her dreams. "Denounced" means "condemned." The passage doesn't talk of dreams condemning Fiona to anything, so this is wrong. "Enraptured" means "captivated." Given the amount of study Fiona has put into dreams, she can accurately be described as "captivated" by them.

For the second blank, the passage states that Fiona is convinced that dreams have logical impetuses, even if they aren't clear. "Debonair" means "charming." Having charming dreams would not prevent Fiona from understanding them. "Gentile" means "amiable." Having amiable dreams would not prevent Fiona from understanding them, either. "Abstruse" means "perplexing." This makes sense.

Fiona would have a hard time understanding perplexing dreams.

For the third blank, the passage does not seem confident that the experts are really experts. It even goes so far as to put "experts" in quotations to show Fiona's doubts. "Solemn" means "serious." If Fiona is referring to the experts ironically, she would not be calling them serious. "Guileless" means "honest." Again, if Fiona is referring to the experts in the field ironically then she would not be calling them honest. "Charlatans" means "fakes." If Fiona is referring to the experts in the field ironically then she clearly considers them fakes.

61.   *enigmatic, exorbitant* and *exhaustive*

The paragraph says that it is difficult to locate the many organisms living in the ocean because of the space they have to live in. Our lack of experience with them gives the organisms a secretive quality. "Haughty" means "proud." Being rarely seen would not cause aquatic life to be "proud." "Vituperative" means "offensive." Again, being rarely seen would not make aquatic life offensive. "Enigmatic" means "mysterious." This accurately describes how aquatic life would appear to humans if we've rarely or never seen them before.

The second sentence stresses the sheer size of the ocean and describes how this size is perceived in terms of searching for marine life. It must be considered excessively large for that purpose. "Coquettish" means "demure." This personality trait does not explain how the size of the ocean would be perceived by those looking for life within it. "Ardent" means "zealous." Once again, this word does not describe how the ocean would be perceived by those trying to find life within it. We are left with "Exorbitant." This word means "excessive." This describes exactly how one would feel about the size of the ocean when searching it for life.

The last sentence stresses how understanding every aspect of marine life is necessary in order to attain a certain type of understanding about the ocean. This "certain type" of understanding must be complete understanding if it requires understanding everything, including microscopic organisms. "Diminutive" means "small." A small understanding would not require knowing how every microscopic organism functions within the ocean. "Reticent" means "shy." A "shy" understanding does not make sense. "Exhaustive" means "complete." This makes sense. A complete understanding of marine life would require knowing how everything, including microscopic organisms, function within the ocean.

62.   *vocations* and *exactitude*

The first blank talks about how there are "things" that fall under the heading of biotechnology that one wouldn't expect. We want a word that describes what these "things" might be. By reading further into the passage we see various jobs listed – brewers of alcohol and agricultural developers. Therefore, we want a word that describes a job. "Verisimilitudes" means "truths." This does not describe a field of work and therefore is incorrect. "Denigrations" means "defamations." These are insults and not fields of work. "Vocations" means "life's work." This describes the jobs that unexpectedly fall into the category of "biotechnology."

The last sentence is comparing what you would expect to fall under the heading of "biotechnology" (medical procedures of a certain quality) with what you wouldn't expect ("rough-and-tumble" jobs). Therefore, we want a word that would contrast with the "rough-and-tumble" description given to the latter group of jobs. "Unsophistication" means "lack of refinement." This relates to "rough-and-tumble" and therefore is incorrect. "Fallacy" means "misconception." This word does not contrast the scientific procedures with the "rough-and-tumble" jobs. "Exactitude" means "precision." This word contrasts nicely with "rough-and-tumble."

63. *inhospitable* and *foil*

Desolate landscapes and small populations do not sound particularly promising, and the word missing in the first sentence must reflect that. *Germane* means *relevant*, which is not the best way to describe whether or not a location is suitable for business (in fact, *germane* more commonly refers to comments or topics). *Morbid*, on the other hand, is too extreme; it means *unwholesome* or *gruesome*. The correct answer is *inhospitable*, which simply means *unwelcoming* or *unfavorable*.

In order to fill in the second blank, you need to read the passage all the way through to the end. We are told that South Dakota has very low taxes; presumably, since the author sees fit to mention it, this is one reason why it is a good place to start a business. Places with high taxes, then, are probably not conducive to succeeding in business, and the missing word should reflect that. *Obviate* means *to anticipate and prevent*, but does not quite work in this sentence; it is generally used when the thing being prevented is unnecessary, impractical, harmful, etc. *Lampoon* is appropriately negative, but does not make very much sense in this context; it means *to ridicule* or *to satirize*. The correct answer is *foil*, which means *to impede* or *to prevent the success of*.

64. *belligerent*

This sentence is about the military successes of Ghengis Khan and the Mongols; the missing word could mean something like *aggressive*, but it could also just mean *effective*. The best way to solve it, then, is by process of elimination. *Rancorous* means *spiteful* or *maliciously resentful*; even for a description of a military leader, it is a rather strong word, and one that implies a moral judgment, so you should eliminate it. *Timorous* (*fearful* or *timid*) clearly will not work. *Disingenuous* means *insincere*; again, it suggests moral condemnation, but more importantly, there is nothing in this passage about Ghengis Khan's honesty or lack thereof - eliminate it. *Erratic* means *unpredictable* or *having no definite course*. It is probably not the best description of a successful leader, so you should check to see if the other remaining choice makes more sense. *Belligerent* means *warlike*, and is the correct answer.

65. *impervious to* and *forestall*

We know from the word *though* that the missing word in the first sentence must in some way contrast with the fact that women are unlikely to have X-linked disorders; check the answers and see if there is a word that makes sense, given this. *Inclined to* will not work, because there is no contradiction between the idea that women are *not inclined to genetic disorders* and the fact that they are not susceptible to X-linked conditions. *Intransigent* means *uncompromising* or *inflexible* and generally describes someone's attitude; it is hard to see what being *uncompromising towards* a disease means, or how it has anything to do with one's susceptibility - eliminate it. The correct answer is *impervious to* (*invulnerable* or *incapable of being injured*).

To fill in the second blank, notice that we are told that women have a *normal gene* that produces *clotting factors*. Even if you don't know exactly what clotting factors are, you can almost certainly deduce that they make blood clot (and therefore prevent *life-threatening bleeds*). *Engender* is nearly the opposite of what we want; it means *to produce* or *cause*. *To mollify* means *to soften* or *to mitigate*; it is a better answer, since it means something like *to make less severe*, but it is more often used in the context of feelings rather than physical injuries. *To forestall* is the better option; it means *to prevent* or *to anticipate*.

66. *partisan, soporific* and *eschew*

To solve the first blank, you will need to use process of elimination to find the best answer. *Rancorous*, or *spiteful*, is a bit extreme; in the absence of further information, we should give even a politician the benefit of the doubt and assume he doesn't want to elicit actual hostility. *Indigenous* is not a very good choice either; it means *originating in a particular region*. Given the political context, *partisan* (*partial to a particular person or party*) makes the most sense.

We are then told that the candidate was probably *disappointed* by the speech's effect. If his goal was in fact to stir up partisan feelings, he would likely have been gratified by an *incendiary* (*tending to arouse or inflame*) effect - eliminate this choice. *Noxious* is probably too strong a word to be warranted in this context; it means *harmful* or *corrupting*. *Soporific,* which means *tending to cause sleep*, is the best answer.

In the final sentence, we are told that the candidate's speech was characterized by *reasoned argument*. To fill in the final blank, then, we need to find a word that will make the sentence read something like *the politician avoided inflammatory taglines in favor of reasoned arguments*. *Abhor* (*to loathe* or *to detest utterly*) is too strong a word, and does not really work with the sentence structure - one does not generally *abhor* something *in favor of* something else. *Preclude* is also not quite what we need; it means *to make impossible*. *To eschew*, however, means *to abstain* or *to avoid* and is the correct answer.

67.   *tractable, repudiate* and *abide by*

You need to read at least the second sentence before attempting to fill in the first. We are told that we like to think of ourselves as firm in our beliefs, when in truth those beliefs are easily swayed. The first blank, therefore, must refer to this susceptibility to external suggestion. *Dogmatic* is nearly the opposite; it means *opinionated* or *asserting opinions in a doctrinaire manner*. *Fatuous* (*foolish*) is better, but is a bit too judgmental - eliminate it. You are left with *tractable*, which means *easily managed* or *yielding*. In order to fill in the last two blanks, you need to have some sense of what the sentence as a whole is saying; the gist seems to be that participants in the Asch study misjudged the length of a line *in the interests of conformity*. For the first blank, then, we need a word that means something like *ignore*.

Vituperate (*vilify* or *berate*) makes no sense in this context; there is no suggestion that the participants actively criticized their sensory perceptions. You have probably heard the phrase *garner evidence* before, but do not be led astray; *to garner* means *to gather*, which does not work here. *To repudiate*, on the other hand, works well; it means *to reject* or *to refuse to acknowledge*.

Finally, we need a word that means something like *agree with* to fill in the last blank. *To preclude* means *to make impossible*, while *to quibble with* means *to make trivial objections*; neither makes sense in this context. *Abide by* (*to act in accord with* or *to submit to*) is the correct answer.

68.   *ubiquitous*

In this sentence we are looking for a word that will contradict the idea that radiation is *out of the ordinary* - perhaps *common* or something similar. *Ineffable* (*incapable of being expressed*) has to do with whether or not something can be described, which is not in question here - eliminate it. *Nebulous* means *hazy* or *indistinct*. It is not a very good choice, unless perhaps you imagine that it is hard to avoid *indistinct* things. In any case, it has nothing to do with being *out of the ordinary*, so you should be able to eliminate it. You can rule out *quiescent* for similar reasons; it might be hard to avoid something *dormant* simply because you don't know that it is there, but what would this mean in the context of radiation, and what does it have to do with being uncommon? If you can't answer these questions, you should eliminate the word. *Foolproof* means *never-failing* and is more commonly used to describe plans or ideas - eliminate it. The correct answer is *ubiquitous*, which means *present everywhere*.

69.   *indigenous* and *deleterious*

As its name should tell you, an invasive species is an organism that is not native to a particular place but has moved in and is disrupting the local ecosystem. It is a threat to local plants and animals, so the first blank probably means something like native. Inveterate means firmly established by long continuance, but it more commonly refers to feelings, practices, or even diseases than it does to plants or animals. Pugnacious means quarrelsome or combative; there is nothing in the passage to suggest that native species are unusually aggressive, so you should eliminate it. This leaves you with indigenous, which means originating in and characteristic of a particular region and is the best answer.

To fill in the second blank, you simply need a general sense of the passage's point - that invasive species are harmful. Covert means concealed or secret. It is clear from the passage, however, that at least some invasive species have a very obvious effect on the environment (see, for example, the description of the emerald ash borer), so you should be able to eliminate this choice. Perfidious, on the other hand, is too strong a word; it means treacherous or disloyal and implies a malicious intent that insects presumably do not have. Deleterious, or injurious, is the best choice.

70. *trenchant*

We are told that the teacher was impressed by the student's comments, so presumably they were insightful. Urbane is probably an overstatement; it means reflecting elegance or sophistication. Pedantic, on the other hand, means ostentatious in one's learning, and has negative connotations - eliminate it. An equivocal, or deliberately ambiguous, answer would probably not impress the teacher, particularly because it implies an intent to deceive. Likewise, a *loquacious* observation is not particularly praiseworthy; it means *characterized by excessive talk*. The best answer is *trenchant* (*incisive* or *keen*).

71. *catalyst, heinous* and *opprobrium*

The first sentence informs us that the death of Hu Yaobang caused the protests, so we are looking for a word that describes something that causes something else. An antidote (something that prevents or counteracts injurious or unwanted effects) causes improvement, but that clearly will not work in this sentence, which describes events culminating in a massacre. Imbroglio will also not work; it means a misunderstanding or an intricate and perplexing affair, and better describes the circumstances following Hu Yaobang's death than the death itself. The correct answer is catalyst, which means a thing that precipitates an event or change.

As for the final two blanks, you should be able to glean from the rest of the passage that the government responded to the protests in a particularly savage way that was probably not received well in other countries, so you should be looking for words in keeping with this. Redoubtable means formidable, and it often implies respect, which is clearly not appropriate here - eliminate it. Dubious means questionable and is also not a good choice; there is no question that the government's actions were unethical. You are left with heinous (hateful or totally reprehensible).

As for the last blank, encomium would certainly not be an appropriate response; it means a formal expression of high praise. Sanctimony is also a bad fit; it means pretended, affected, or hypocritical religious devotion, righteousness, etc. Opprobrium (reproach or censure) seems a quite likely reaction, however, and is the correct answer.

72. *cumbersome, diaphanous* and *lithe*

In the first sentence, we learn that female dancers' corsets, hoops, and high heels prevented them from taking center stage - probably because the costumes were simply too difficult to move in. Disheveled does not make very much sense; there is no indication that the dancers' costumes were routinely untidy or disordered, and even if they were, couldn't they simply fix them? Maladroit is not a good fit because it usually describes people or their actions, not clothing; it means inept or awkward. Cumbersome (burdensome or unwieldy) is the correct answer.

To fill in the last two blanks, think about the way this passage describes ballet dancers; they act the part of nymphs and spirits, they float effortlessly, and they are ethereal. Your answers need to mesh with these descriptions. Dulcet means soothing or melodious; it usually refers to sound, so it is probably not the best description of costumes. Meretricious (tawdry or based on pretense) is too negative a word. Diaphanous is the best answer; it means very sheer and light and fits in well with the passage's depiction of ballet dancers.

Brittle (easily damaged or destroyed) will not work well for the last blank; dancers' bodies may seem fragile, but the connotations of brittle are too negative for a passage that otherwise describes the dancers in flattering terms. Supine does not make sense; a dancer could hardly remain inactive or lying on her back. The best answer is lithe, which means supple or limber.

73.   *conspicuous*

20 percent seems fairly significant, and the missing word probably reflects this. Temperate will not work; the amount of money in question does not suggest moderate or self-restrained behavior on the part of the teenagers. Nebulous means hazy or indistinct and does not make sense here, given that we are actually given an exact percentage. Ignominious (disgraceful or contemptible) is too strong a word - eliminate it. You may know that impecunious has something to do with money but do not be tricked into choosing it; it means having little or no money and does not make sense in this context. The correct answer is conspicuous (striking or noticeable).

74.   *harbinger* and *corroboration*

The statement that tornadoes are unpredictable is presented as counterevidence to an assertion made in the first sentence. This should clue you in to the kind of word you need for the first blank - specifically, a word implying that green skies predict tornadoes. Propagation means multiplication or dissemination and does not really make sense in this context - eliminate it. An incursion is an invasion or a harmful inroad, which still does not quite capture the notion that green skies precede tornadoes. The correct answer is harbinger (an omen).

As for the second blank, we are told that even radar is not an entirely reliable indicator of tornadoes,

and that eyewitness accounts are also needed; the missing word must mean something like confirmation. Reciprocity means mutual exchange; it is somewhat awkward here, particularly given that we are not told that the eyewitness accounts require radar confirmation. Approbation means or commendation or official approval, and is again a bit out of place here; it implies an approving attitude rather than simple confirmation. The correct answer is corroboration, which means confirmation or authentication.

75.   *reprobate, tenuous and maligning*

The first sentence describes Richard III, at least in Shakespeare, as murderous. Clearly we need a word that implies condemnation of some sort. Mendicant won't work; it simply means beggar, which a king is unlikely to be in any case. An iconoclast is a person who attacks traditional beliefs or institutions, and the passage gives us no reason to suspect Richard of subversive activities; regardless of whether or not he killed his nephews, he presumably did not attack the monarchy as an institution. Reprobate (a depraved or unprincipled person) is the correct answer.

Moving on to the next blank, we know from the use of however that the historians mentioned in the sentence must doubt Shakespeare's portrayal of Richard; they presumably believe that the evidence against him is weak. Whimsical means fanciful or given to fanciful notions; it is not normally used in the context of something as serious as evidence. Quotidian means ordinary or commonplace - something that would presumably have no effect on the veracity of the evidence. Tenuous means thin or unsubstantiated and is the best answer. F

Finally, in order to fill in the last blank, we need to find a word that deals with Shakespeare's handling of Richard's character. Renovating will obviously not work; someone who renovates a person's reputation would be restoring it to good condition. Commemorating also has connotations that are too positive for this context; to commemorate means to honor the memory of. Maligning (slandering or speaking ill of) is the correct answer.

76. *restive*

As you should be able to glean from the use of the word forced, the children are probably not happy to be inside; the correct answer needs to describe a plausible effect of keeping kids inside against their will for several days. Boorish means unmannered or crude. Unless the speaker in this sentence is particularly snobby, it does not make a lot of sense to describe children this way, given that no one expects them to be models of propriety - eliminate it. Phlegmatic (calm or not easily excited) is an even less apt description of the average child - particularly one who has been inside for a week. Gregarious means sociable. It is hard to see what connection this could have to staying inside; if anything, being cut off from other people for an extended period of time would seem likely to make one less sociable. Finally, feckless means ineffective or lazy. Again, it is a strange adjective to apply to children, who are not expected to be as productive as adults. Restive, on the other hand, fits well and is the correct answer; it means restless or stubborn.

77. *mundane* and *tenacity*

The use of the word even implies that the missing word goes one step beyond humble in describing these companies beginnings. Frugal is not entirely out of the realm of possibility - it means economical in use or expenditure - but ask yourself if it works in the context of the passage as a whole. The sentence has nothing to do with money, so frugal is probably not the best answer. Bogus, on the other hand, is unwarrantedly negative; we have no reason to think that these companies have origins that are counterfeit or not genuine. Mundane, however, works well with the second half of the sentence; it means banal or earthly, which a rice cooker surely is.

As for the second blank, we are looking for a quality - distinct from vision - that could help get a business off the ground. It is not inconceivable that presumption (bold or insolent behavior) could help a young business survive, but it is a somewhat negative that the sentence as a whole does not justify. You should eliminate sophistry for the same reasons; it means a tricky but generally fallacious method of reasoning. This leaves you with tenacity (perseverance), which is the correct answer.

78. *contentious*, *brash* and *condone*

You will definitely want to read the entire passage before attempting to tackle the first blank. The key information here is that some people believe that the language used in victimology risks blaming the victim. It would seem, then, that victimology sometimes deals with controversial or touchy subjects, and we need a word that reflects this. Salacious is not a good choice; although some people might take a salacious (lustful or obscene) interest in certain crimes, this passage does not deal with that. Propitious will not work either; it means favorable or auspicious. The best answer is contentious, which means characterized by argument or controversy.

Where the second blank is concerned, we are looking for a word describing behavior that might catch the attention of a criminal. Timorous seems unlikely. While it is not out of the question that a criminal might target someone who seems fearful or timid, such is surely not the case in most crimes. Fulsome is too strong a word, even given the controversial nature of the term victim precipitation; it means offensive to good taste or sickening. The correct answer is brash, which means impertinent or, in this case, impetuous.

Finally, we need a word that means something like excuse for the final blank - excusing the crime is the natural consequence of blaming the victim. To provoke (to anger or to induce) might describe what, according to the theory of victim precipitation, the victim does, but it is not a good fit here - eliminate it. Rescind is too formal a word for this context; implicitly excusing the crime is not the same as officially invalidating or revoking it. You are left with condone, which means to disregard or to give tacit approval to.

79.   *renowned* and *poignant*

If L'Orfeo is regarded as the first opera, it probably enjoys a fairly prestigious reputation. Incongruous (out of keeping or place or not harmonious in character) will not work, because one would expect the first opera to enjoy *a reputation*. *Unscathed* (*unharmed*) is not a good choice either, because it implies that L'Orfeo has escaped some threat to its reputation, which the sentence does not mention. *Renowned* (*celebrated* or *distinguished*) is the correct answer.

In order to fill in the second blank, you do not need to be familiar with the story of Orpheus. The brief description given to you should allow you to immediately eliminate *droll*; if a story involving a trip to the underworld were somehow *whimsically humorous*, the author would definitely make note of it. Given the respectful tone of the passage, you can also rule out *maudlin*, which means *foolishly sentimental*. The correct answer is *poignant*, which means *affecting* or *moving the emotions*.

80.   *phlegmatic, sluggard* and *abstain from*

As this passage implies, the sloth has a reputation for being slow and lazy, and the first missing word will reflect that. Fulsome is too negative for the neutral and descriptive tone of the passage; it means offensive to good taste or sickening. Lugubrious means mournful or gloomy and has nothing to do with the subject of the passage. This leaves you with phlegmatic, which means not easily excited to action or display of emotion and is the correct answer.

Given this, the second blank must refer to a lazy or inactive person. Virago means an ill-tempered, scolding woman - eliminate it. Libertine is similarly irrelevant; it means a person who is morally or sexually unrestrained. Sluggard, however, fits perfectly; it refers to a person who is habitually inactive or lazy.

Finally, we know from the rest of the passage that sloths do not move frequently, so they must avoid physical activity. Inveigh against does not make sense; sloths do not protest strongly against physical activity, they simply refrain from it. There is also no indication that sloths go through an active period, so it cannot be that they wean themselves off (withdraw from) physical activity. The best answer is abstain from, which means to hold oneself back voluntarily.

81.   *pellucid* and *august*

If the speaker was charmed by the Mediterranean, the missing word must be positive. For this reason, you can immediately rule out turbid (clouded because of stirred-up sediment). Quiescent means quiet or motionless. Although this is not a negative description, we are more likely to admire the stillness of a pond or lake than we are that of a sea or ocean. Pellucid is a better answer; it means translucent or limpid. The keys to filling in the second blank are the words grandeur, stately, and imposing. We need a word that conveys a similar sense of majesty. Irrevocable does not, and in any case it makes little sense to describe a relic as unable to be repealed or annulled. Portentous (ominous or momentous) is better, but often hints at an underlying threat or danger that does not make sense in this context. August (venerable or inspiring reverence) is the best answer.

82.   *confounded*

As the second half of the sentence informs you, light has some unusual - and confusing - properties. The missing word could mean something as simple as *interested*, but it is possible that even these thinkers have found the nature of light perplexing, so we could also be looking for a word meaning *confused*. In either case, *placated* does not make sense, because even if scientists could be *appeased* by questions about light, why would they need to be appeased in the first place? *Fettered* is too strong a word; it means *confined* or *restrained*. *To implicate* means *to show to be involved in* or *to connect* or *relate to intimately* - eliminate it. Finally, *enervated* means *weakened* or *deprived of strength*; clearly scientists cannot have been too *weakened* by these questions, or they would never have made any progress. Eliminate it.

The best answer is *confounded* (*bewildered*).

83. *trifling, inadvertent* and *sagacious*

The use of the word *seemingly* suggests that the details that *make all the difference* do not seem particularly important, so you should look for a word that means something like *insignificant*. It would no doubt be helpful to have an eye for *disparate* details - that is, details that appear *distinct* or *dissimilar* - in case they end up being related after all, but that is not what this sentence is about - eliminate it. *Spurious* means *not genuine, authentic,* or *true*. It does not make sense in this context, particularly given the later discussion of color; color can't be *inauthentic*. *Trifling* is the best answer; it means *trivial* or *insignificant*.

To fill in the second blank, we need a word that in some way contrasts with *powerful*, and that describes the effects of color on a person's mood. *Nugatory* means *of no real value*. It does somewhat contrast with *powerful*, but it also makes no sense in this sentence; if color can be an *effective tool* in marketing, clearly it does have value. *Salutary* is too specific; it means *healthful* or *wholesome*, and one can easily imagine a situation in which color could have a negative effect on one's mood. This leaves you with *inadvertent*, which works well with the notion that color could be written off as a *trifling detail*; it means *unintentional*.

Finally, the last blank requires a word that describes the kind of businessman who uses color effectively - *savvy* or something similar, perhaps. You may know that *impecunious* has something to do with money and be tempted to pick it for this reason - don't. It means *penniless,* which is more or less irrelevant to this sentence, unless the businessman is so poor that he can't afford a bucket of paint. *Officious* (*meddlesome* or *aggressive in offering one's services*) does not make sense either; the businessman in question is presumably looking out for himself rather than offering to help others. The correct answer is *sagacious* (*shrewd*).

84. *alacrity*

In this question we are looking for a way of eating that might offend people with *impeccable manners*. *Efficacy* is probably not the correct answer. To begin with, it means *effectiveness,* which is not a word we usually associate with eating. It is also hard to imagine why anyone would object to *effective eating,* providing it was done politely - eliminate it. *Decorum* is the opposite of what we are looking for; it means *dignified propriety* and is precisely the sort of thing that would impress people who emphasize table manners. You can eliminate *adroitness* for the same reasons you eliminated *efficacy*; it means *skill* or *resourcefulness. Temperance* means *moderation or self-restraint* and would, again, probably go over well with the guests described in the sentence. This leaves you with *alacrity* (*briskness* or *readiness*). Eating quickly could very well offend people who insist on proper table manners, so this is the best answer.

85. *plethora*

The fact that Petra was located on a trade route, as well as the fact that its architecture apparently utilizes at least two column styles, suggests that it was probably influenced by a variety of cultures. You can, therefore, immediately rule out *dearth*, which means *scarcity* or *lack. Imprecation* is irrelevant in this context; it means *a curse*. Eliminate it. Both *travesty* (*a debased likeness* or *imitation*) and *adulteration* (*debasement*) imply that the architecture of Petra is merely a corruption of other cultural styles. Given that the tone of this passage is in no way negative, you can eliminate both of these words. The correct answer is *plethora*, which means *abundance* or *excess*.

86. *substantiate*

It is important to note that this sentence is discussing the *hypothesized age* rather than simply *the age*. This means that the scientists already have a guess, and are merely trying to confirm it. It is for this reason that you can rule out *discern*, which means *to perceive* or *to recognize. To correlate* means *to bring into mutual* or *reciprocal relation*; it is hard to see what this could have to do with this sentence, particularly since there is no mention of anything the hypothesized age could be correlated with. Eliminate it. It is unlikely that the scientists would be trying to *gainsay* - or *dispute* or *contradict* - their own hypothesis, so you can eliminate this as well. *To palliate* means *to alleviate* or *to extenuate* and is clearly out of place in this context. The correct answer is *substantiate* (*to establish by proof* or *evidence*).

87.   *ramifications* and *precipitate*

The gist of the first sentence seems to be that studying viruses is important because its findings may affect other areas of medicine - the missing word probably means something like implications. Proscriptions is probably too specific; it means prohibitions, and while it is not inconceivable that a medical study might lead to some prohibitions or restrictions, this particular passage mentions nothing of the kind. You can eliminate exigencies (a state that demands prompt remedy or action or the need intrinsic to a situation) for the same reason. The best answer is ramifications (outgrowths or consequences).

The second half of the passage deals with the potentially harmful consequences of otherwise innocuous viruses, which, we are told, have been linked to certain forms of cancer. It would be unusual to use the word truncate in the context of a disease, but the context makes it a poor choice regardless; it means to shorten, which, when speaking of cancer, would be a good thing. To attenuate means to weaken or reduce in force - again, a desirable effect in the context of a disease. This leaves you with precipitate, which means to hasten the occurrence of.

88.   *abhorred, mandated* and *immaculate*

As the first sentence of this passage implies, incest is taboo in many contemporary cultures, so you should look for a word that expresses strong censure or disapproval. Venial means not seriously wrong or excusable and is a near antonym. Ancillary will also not work; it means subordinate or auxiliary and would imply that society approved of, or at least tolerated, incest. The correct answer is abhorred (detested).

By contrast, the second blank requires a word that means something stronger than tolerated; if brother-sister marriages were actually used by the royal family for a specific purpose, they must have been approved of or even required. You can, therefore, rule out condoned (to overlook or to excuse). Rectified (remedied or righted) will not work in this sentence either, as it implies that brother-sister marriages were seen as a problem to be fixed. This leaves you with mandated, which means authorized or required.

To fill in the last blank, you will need to think about what the purpose of marrying within the royal family might have been. You can probably guess that the Egyptian royal family, like most royalty throughout history, wanted their line to remain untainted by *inferior* blood, so the missing word probably means something like *pure. Omnipotent* will not work because the missing word is modifying *bloodline* rather than *family*; the family almost certainly wished to remain *unlimited in power*, but it does not make much sense to refer to the bloodline in this way. *Empyreal* is also slightly off the mark; it means *pertaining to the sky* or *celestial*. As a matter of fact, the Egyptian royals were considered divine, but since this information is not provided in the passage itself, it is best to eliminate this answer. The correct answer is *immaculate*, or *free from spot or stain*.

89.   *superfluous* and *formidable*

Even if you don't know what vestigial means, you should be able to figure out that the missing word must mean something like useless or unnecessary, because it is meant to contrast with the word valuable. Apocryphal means either false or of doubtful authorship or authenticity. It is mainly used to describe stories, and in any case, vestigial organs or behaviors aren't false - just unnecessary. Exiguous means scanty, meager, or small; given that there is no indication in the passage that vestigial organs or reflexes have dwindled or weakened in any way, it is probably not the best choice. The correct answer is superfluous (excessive or unnecessary).

To fill in the second blank, think about why appearing larger might help an animal faced with a predator - perhaps it makes the animal look more threatening. It is not clear why bristling fur would make an animal appear more obsequious (fawning or deferential), and even if it did, this would probably not help ward off a predator. Impassive is a slightly better choice - an animal that appears unmoved or calm in the face of a predator might make that predator think twice about its chances - but what does this have to do with looking larger? The best answer is formidable (causing fear or of discouraging strength or size).

90. *reviled, lurid* and *obfuscate*

We know from the word although that the first half of the first sentence is meant to contrast with the second half, so if The Picture of Dorian Gray is now an acclaimed work, it must have been ignored or even criticized at the time it was published. Vaunted, which means boasted of, is close to the opposite of what we are looking for, then. Expunged is better, but still not a good choice; it means erased or wiped out, which the novel clearly was not, given that it is still in existence today. The best answer is reviled, which means vilified or disparaged.

We don't have much to go on for the second blank, except that the novel was taken as an account of moral depravity; we can assume, at least, that the missing adjective is nothing complimentary. Histrionic, which means deliberately affected or overly dramatic, is somewhat plausible, but don't pick it until you've read through all the choices. Insipid is probably not correct; it means vapid or bland, which just doesn't seem a strong enough description for a supposedly immoral story. Lurid, on the other hand, ties in with the book's perceived immorality and is therefore the best choice; it means gruesome, shocking, or terrible in intensity.

The final blank clearly deals with the effect of social climate on the reception of a piece of art. Emblazon does not seem like a very good choice; it means to decorate with brilliant colors or to proclaim, whereas this passage is about the lack of recognition Dorian Gray received as a result of its social context. Atrophy (to affect with atrophy, which means degeneration, decline, or disuse) will not work either, unless you believe that social climate can affect the actual value (i.e. not the perceived value) of something. The correct answer is *obfuscate*, which means *to make obscure or unclear*.

91. *lambent*

Given that this sentence is discussing how brilliant the colors of a sunset appear, the missing adjective could very well mean something like vivid, bright, or simply beautiful. Fervid conveys the idea of intensity, but it is a better description of people or feelings than it is of colors; it means heated or vehement in spirit or burning. Plangent means having a loud deep sound or resonant and mournful. Even when it is used in the latter sense, it almost always refers to sounds - eliminate it. Do not be tricked into choosing crepuscular; it means of or pertaining to twilight, which is not the same as sunset. Winsome, again, is more usually associated with people than colors; it means winning or sweetly charming. The best answer is lambent (softly bright or glowing).

92. *vociferous* and *unpalatable*

For the first blank, we are looking for a word that, along with widespread, could describe objections - perhaps a word that conveys the intensity of the objections, like vehement or strenuous. Bombastic is probably not a good choice because of its negative connotations; we have no reason to believe that the author of this passage views the objections as high-flown or pretentious. Moribund (in a dying state or stagnant) contradicts the notion that the objections are significant enough that the governor incurred criticism for ignoring them. Vociferous (vocal or clamorous) is the best answer.

The second blank presumably requires a word like unpleasant - that is, a word that will explain the existence of widespread objections. Clearly the laws are not imminent (impending) because they are already in place. Execrable is simply too strong a word; it is difficult to imagine the governor defending his decision by acknowledging that the laws were utterly detestable. Unpalatable is a safer choice, because it simply means unpleasant or disagreeable.

93.   *forestall, onerous* and *wary*

Most people would probably want something done about the *worst effects* of climate change - or any other problem, for that matter. To fill in the first blank, therefore, we need a word that means something like address or mitigate. Descry is not a good choice; it is not enough to discern or perceive the worst effects, and it is not clear how reducing emissions would accomplish this in any case. It is also hard to imagine how one could propitiate (appease or conciliate) climate change - generally speaking, only people are capable of being appeased. Forestall (prevent or anticipate) is the correct answer.

For the second blank, we need a word that explains why the companies mentioned in the passage feel they cannot comply with the law. Meretricious does not make sense; surely even a law that is tawdry or based on pretense can be followed, and in any case, there is nothing in the passage suggesting that the program is simply for show. Amorphous is slightly more plausible. It could very well be difficult to comply with a law that is unorganized or lacking definite shape. However, the final sentence should tell you that onerous (burdensome) is a better choice; concrete companies feel that cutting emissions is essentially impracticable.

The final blank requires a word that describes the relationship between concrete makers and the new law. There is no reason, based on this passage, to think that they are more cognizant (aware) of the law than any other company affected by it. Devoid simply does not make sense in this sentence; it means *not possessing*, and laws are not generally things that can be *possessed*. This leaves you with *wary* (*cautious towards* or *leery of*), which is the correct answer.

94.   *beguiled*

In this sentence, we are looking for a word describing an emotional state that something awe-inspiring might evoke. It is possible that something awe-inspiring could cause someone to be perturbed, but this would be slightly redundant coming after repulsed; the word sublime has basically positive connotations, so the missing word presumably describes an emotion that counterbalances the repulsion already mentioned. Eviscerated is even more unlikely; even if we take it metaphorically, a landscape that disembowels those who see it does not sound appealing in any way. To transcend means to rise above or go beyond or to surpass. It is quite likely that a sublime landscape might also appear transcendent, but given that this passage focuses more on the spectator's reactions to the landscape rather than the landscape itself, it is not a good fit here. Galvanized is also not a good choice; if the people in question were startled into sudden activity, we would almost certainly be told what it was they were suddenly inspired to do. The correct answer is beguiled, which means charmed or captivated.

95.   *dispassionate* and *jibe with*

In the first sentence, we are looking for a word that describes observations in a way that contrasts with judgments based on unconscious beliefs and biases - that is, a word that means something like unbiased. Chary means cautious or wary and is often followed by of. It is not the best choice, but if you are unsure, set it aside and see if there is a more likely answer. Momentous (of great importance) won't work; if we truly believed our judgments were momentous, this in and of itself would be a self-serving bias. The best choice is dispassionate, which means impartial or calm.

As for the second blank, the fact that attractive people appear to be given preferential treatment suggests that we see physical appearance as an indication of overall intelligence and morality. The word we choose needs to reflect this. To ascribe to means to credit or attribute. It is a good description of our actions - we unconsciously ascribe a person's looks to his overall character - but it does not work in this particular sentence. Purport to is also slightly off the mark; it means to profess or to present the appearance of being, but it is generally followed by a verb rather than by a noun (something purports to do or be something). The correct answer is jibe with, which means to be in harmony with or to agree with.

96.   *nonplussed*

If the *average person* only knows about three phases of matter, and the other phases of matter are *bizarre*, people would probably be *surprised* to learn about these other phases. *Contrite* doesn't make sense; why would someone be *remorseful* or *penitent* to learn about other phases of matter? *Saturnine* means *gloomy* or *taciturn*, which would surely be an extreme reaction to learning something new, even if it means your previous beliefs were mistaken. You can eliminate *dispirited* (*discouraged* or *dejected*) for the same reason. *Livid* would be even more of an overreaction; it means *enraged*. *Nonplussed* (*puzzled*) is the best answer.

97.   *moribund, torpid* and *foster*

If virtually all efforts at community outreach had ceased, the group is probably not doing well - look for a word that reflects this. However badly the group is doing, however, it is not chimerical (unreal); it definitely exists if new members have joined it and are making plans to rehabilitate it. The group may be superannuated (antiquated or too old for use), but the fact that it is experiencing difficult times does not in and of itself imply that it is very old or obsolete. The best answer is moribund, which means in a dying state or stagnant.

To fill in the next blank, we need to look for a word that could conceivably describe the leadership of such a group - ineffective perhaps? Frowzy is probably not correct; it means slovenly or musty, which has no bearing on how well the group is functioning. Stringent is slightly more plausible, but would not necessarily cause problems for the group; strict or exacting leadership could be harmful if taken too far, but it could potentially accomplish a great deal as well. Torpid (inactive or slow) fits in well with moribund and is the correct answer.

Finally, the last sentence implies that the new recruits hope to stir up new interest in the group, so we need a word that means something like elicit or incite. To perpetrate means to commit or to execute and has generally negative connotations (as in, perpetrate a crime) - it is out of place here. Make sure that you do not mix up convoke and evoke; the former means to call together (as in, to convoke an assembly), while the latter means to elicit or draw forth. The best answer is foster (to promote the growth of or to encourage).

98.   *cursory, dynamic* and *harrowing*

If van Gogh has a *highly distinctive style*, it probably does not require much time or effort to get a feel for it; the sentence is probably supposed to mean something like *even the idlest...* or *even the briefest...* so look for an adjective along those lines. *Perspicacious* (*having keen mental judgment* or *discerning*) will not work, given that it implies a good deal of knowledge. A *jaundiced* viewpoint would be unlikely to help you learn anything new; it is generally best to regard a work of art as objectively as possible, and *jaundiced* means *affected with prejudice*. *Cursory* (*hasty* or *superficial*) is the correct answer.

When working on the second blank, consider the phrases *bold brushstrokes* and *unusual emotional intensity*; whichever adjective we choose to modify *colors* needs to fit into the overall description of van Gogh's painting. Do not pick *incarnadine* simply because it looks like it may have something to do with colors; it can mean either *blood-red* or *flesh-colored*, so you should ask yourself if an artist is likely to paint only in shades of red. Unless neither of the other answers makes sense, this is probably not your best bet - eliminate it. *Funereal* (*mournful* or *dismal*) colors sound as if they might be muted; unless the *emotional intensity* of van Gogh's painting is of a consistently gloomy sort, this is probably not the best choice. The correct answer is *dynamic* (*characterized by force of personality, ambition, energy, new ideas, etc*).

For the last blank, we need to find a word to describe a *struggle with mental illness*. If van Gogh's mental illness was only *affected* (*assumed artificially* or *feigned*), the passage would certainly make note of it. *Iniquitous* (*wicked, sinful*) implies moral condemnation, which is surely unwarranted in the case of an illness. The correct answer is *harrowing*, which means *extremely distressing* or *grievous*.

99.   *precipitous*

Even if you know nothing about the Himalayas, you are told that they have *jagged peaks,* which means that they will have *steep* or *sharp* drops as well. Do not be tricked into picking *nascent* (*beginning to exist or develop*) simply because you are told that the Himalayas are fairly young mountains; it does not make very much sense to describe *drops* this way. *Surreptitious* is too specific; although there may be *secret* or *stealthy* drops, it is unlikely that all of them will be hidden. *Overweening* (*conceited* or *exaggerated*) is generally used to describe a person or an attitude - not a physical object. *Notorious* is a somewhat plausible answer - very steep drops are likely to be *widely and unfavorably known* - but don't pick it until you have read all of the answers. *Precipitous* (*extremely or impassably steep*) is a better choice because it describes the drops themselves rather than an attitude towards them, and therefore better parallels *jagged peaks.*

100.   *tremulous, fulsome* and *confound*

For the first blank, we are looking for a word to describe a kind of beauty that would *suggest extreme fragility*. Perhaps something like *delicate* or *wispy*. There is no reason that *inordinate* (*excessive*) beauty would necessarily imply fragility - eliminate it. *Mincing* is too negative a word for the neutral, even respectful, tone of this passage; it means *affectedly dainty or elegant. Tremulous*, which means *timid* or *quivering,* is the best answer.

As for the second blank, we know from the passage that some butterflies *advertise* their taste *in the hopes that a predator will not make the same mistake twice.* The butterflies must therefore be either poisonous or extremely bad-tasting. An *insidious* taste is not obvious enough to deter a predator; it means *stealthily treacherous* or *operating in an inconspicuous way but actually with grave effect.* And predators might actually seek out an *elusive* (*hard to express or define*) taste, provided it was a pleasant one. The correct answer is *fulsome* (*offensive* or *sickening*).

Finally, we are told that some butterflies deal with predators by sporting *eye-shaped spots* on their wings; these spots probably either frighten or confuse predators. It is not clear how the spots could *placate* (*appease* or *conciliate*) a predator; it is not as if the butterflies are offering up their wings for consumption. Eliminate it. It is even less likely that the spots could *maim* (*mutilate* or *impair*) a predator. You are left with *confound,* which means *to perplex* and is the correct answer.

101.   *proscription* and *contentious*

For the first blank, we obviously need a word that means something like *law* or *prohibition. Litigation* (*judicial proceeding in a court*) has to do with the law, but is not appropriate for this sentence; we need a word that means the ban itself, not what happens when a ban is broken. *Vituperation* (*violent denunciation*) expresses great depth of feeling but is not formal enough; it is easy to imagine someone denouncing something that is perfectly legal. The correct answer is *proscription* (*prohibition* or *the act of prohibiting*).

The key to filling in the second blank is the idea that different societies may define murder differently; as the second half of the passage informs us, someone who takes Buddhism seriously might regard even killing in self-defense as wrong. The definition of the crime, then, is *controversial* or *unclear*. It is going too far to say the definition is *fallacious* (*logically unsound* or *misleading*); the basic idea behind outlawing murder is a good and sound one. Clearly, however, the definition is not *inclusive* (*comprehensive* or *including everything concerned*), because some cultures could have a very restricted notion of what constitutes murder. *Contentious* (*characterized by argument*) is the correct answer.

102. *filial, deference to* and *tenuous*

To fill in the first blank, we need a word that describes the kind of obedience that *all parents expect.* You should be able to rule out *scrupulous* easily; not all parents expect *minutely careful* or *exact* obedience, and in any case, it makes no sense to speak of *degrees* of *exact* obedience. *Reciprocal* (*corresponding* or *given or felt by each toward the other, mutual*) makes even less sense, as it implies that all parents expect to obey their children, at least in some circumstances. The correct answer is *filial*, which simply means *of, pertaining to, or befitting a son or daughter.*

To fill in the second blank, think about what kind of parenting doesn't give children *a chance to exercise their own judgment* - presumably, one where the parents make all of the decisions. Clearly *intransigence towards* (*inflexibility towards*) will not work, because it implies that the children are doing whatever they want, regardless of their parents' orders. *Propensity for* (*natural tendency toward* is also a bad choice. To begin with, we do not normally speak of *absolute propensities* - it is somewhat like saying *absolute leanings*. In any case, the phrase *propensity for parental authority* is awkward and unclear; does it imply, for example, that the parents are naturally skilled at giving orders? If you cannot make sense of a sentence once you have tried out a word, that word is almost certainly incorrect. The best answer is *deference to* (*respectful submission or yielding to*).

Finally, we need a word to describe the *sense of self* possessed by children who grow up in authoritarian households. If they have low self-esteem and are not used to making decisions for themselves, it is a fair bet that they probably do not have a good grasp of who they are or what they want. *Mercurial* (*volatile* or *animated*) is not a completely implausible answer, given that it implies a somewhat unstable sense of self, but its connotations are too positive for this context; the author clearly disapproves of this parenting style and feels it has negative consequences. On the other hand, *dissolute* (*indifferent to moral restraints* or *licentious*) is too judgmental; the author obviously does not regard these children as in any way immoral. You are left with *tenuous* (*thin* or *weak*), which is the correct answer.

103. *apocryphal*

As their name implies, *urban legends* are not the most reliable of stories, and in this sentence, we are looking for an adjective that reflects their *doubtful origins*. Many urban legends probably are *hyperbolic* (*exaggerated*), but because this does not relate directly to their veracity (or lack thereof), you can eliminate it. The word *ephemeral* implies a kind of insubstantiality, but it means *short-lived*, which urban legends clearly are not. *Judicious* is nearly the opposite of what we are looking for; it means *discreet* or *sensible*. And while urban legends are sometimes *prurient* (*characterized by lascivious or lustful thoughts, desires, etc*), this has nothing to do with their origins. The best answer is *apocryphal*, which means *false* or *of doubtful authorship or authenticity.*

104. *disgruntlement, obtrusively* and *barrage*

Most people don't like advertisements, and if they are seeing/hearing 3,000to 5,000 of them per day, they are probably fairly upset - the first missing word should reflect this. Although some commercials might be *edifying* (*instructive* or *beneficial*), this passage clearly focuses on the downsides of advertising rather than the positives - eliminate *edification*. *Trepidation* is too strong a word; consumers are irritated by advertising, but they do not experience *tremulous fear* or *agitation*. The correct answer is *disgruntlement*, which means *discontent* or *sulky dissatisfaction.*

The second missing word probably also focuses on the frustration of consumers - *irritatingly*, perhaps. *Consummately* does not continue with this theme, and it would in any case be redundant coming directly after *effectively* (it means *completely* or *perfectly*). *Nefariously* (*wickedly* or *heinously*) is probably an overstatement; it is better to avoid such strongly condemnatory words unless you have a very compelling reason to believe the passage requires one. This leaves you with *obtrusively* (*obtrusive* means *meddlesome* or *blatant*), which makes sense in the context of the passage without being repetitive.

Finally, we need to find a word to describe the kind of marketing we are exposed to - most likely one that once more draws attention to its prevalence or frequency. "Dearth" clearly will not work; it means *inadequate supply* or *lack*. *Parlance* (*a way of speaking* or an *idiom*) is not particularly relevant to this passage, which focuses on the quantity of ads we are exposed to, not on the kid of language they use. The correct answer is *barrage*, which means *an overwhelming quantity or explosion*, and therefore best conveys the notion that we are constantly subjected to ads of one kind or another.

105.   *gossamer*

The sentence tells you that cirrus clouds are *wispy*, so the missing adjective probably has a similar or related meaning. *Halcyon* is not totally out of the question; it means *calm, tranquil,* or *carefree*, and can be used to describe weather. However, there may be a still better option, so don't pick it yet. *Sinuous* doesn't really work; something that is *wispy* could be *sinuous* (*curvy* or *winding*), but they're not directly related, so in the absence of any other clues in the sentence, it's probably best to eliminate it. *Variegated* is also unlikely, particularly given that clouds generally appear white, and are therefore not *varied in appearance or color*. *Lambent* means *softly glowing*; again, it is possible that clouds might appear *lambent* - particularly during sunrise or sunset - but it isn't really a quality inherent to any particular type of cloud. The best answer is *gossamer*, which means *delicate, light,* or *gauzy*.

106.   *flippant* and *jocular*

For this first blank, we need a word that can describe a sense of humor - preferably one that suggests an *inability to treat any subject seriously*. If anything, we would expect someone who is *erudite* to take things too seriously; it means *learned* or *scholarly*. Someone could have a *raucous* (*harsh* or *rowdy*) sense of humor, but *flippant* (*frivolously disrespectful* or *characterized by levity*) ties in more directly with the notion of taking things seriously (or not, as the case may be).

We most likely need another word meaning *joking* or *funny* for the second blank. *Iconoclastic* is probably too strong a term, even for someone who might be *frivolously disrespectful*; it means *attacking or ignoring cherished beliefs and long-held traditions*. *Equivocal* (*allowing the possibility of several different meanings, especially with intent to deceive*) is not a word usually used to describe jokes, because while jokes do often hinge on double meanings, they are not meant to be deceptive or tricky. The correct answer is *jocular*, which simply means *joking* or *facetious*.

107.   *expedient*

If the traits in question help animals *survive long enough to mate*, they must be advantageous in some way - the missing word is most likely related to this. A trait that is merely *innocuous* (*harmless* or *inoffensive*) is unlikely to actually prove helpful - eliminate it. A *salient* (*prominent* or *conspicuous*) could prove good or bad, and therefore will not work in this context. *Titillating* (*exciting* or *arousing*) traits might attract potential mates, but the meaning is too specific for this passage, which seems to be discussing any and all traits that help an individual survive and reproduce. Don't pick *prolific* (*highly fruitful* or *highly productive*) simply because of the reference to mating; referring to a trait as *prolific* does not make very much sense. The best answer is *expedient* (*fit or suitable for some purpose* or *conducive to advantage or interest*).

108.   *enigmatic, austere* and *fester*

The key to filling in the first blank is too recognize that this passage is primarily about possible explanations for the Salem witch trials. Although the witch trials are somewhat *infamous* (*notorious* or *heinous*), this does not have anything to do with what caused them - eliminate it. *Clandestine* is slightly off the mark; it means *executed with secrecy or deception, especially for purposes of subversion or deception*. Although the witch trials are mysterious, it is not as if anyone is concealing information about them, so you can eliminate this answer as well. The best answer is *enigmatic* (*perplexing* or *mysterious*).

To fill in the second blank, we need a word to describe the *religious climate* at the time of the trials. You may very well know that the residents of Salem were members of the Puritan religion, which is notoriously strict, but even if you don't, you should be able to eliminate the wrong answers fairly easily. It is unlikely, for example, that *vitriolic* (*very caustic, scathing*) is the correct answer; it implies that the Puritans' religious beliefs were based on ill-will and malevolence, which is simply too extreme a statement to make about any religion. *Pristine*, on the other hand, has somewhat positive connotations and is therefore not suited to this context; it means *uncorrupted or unsullied*. The correct answer is *austere*, which means *strict, ascetic*, or *somber*.

Finally, the passage implies that the religious and socio-economic climate of Salem was conducive to *mass hysteria*; we are probably looking for a word that means something like *take root*, or *flourish*. *To convene* means *to cause to assemble*. It is generally used of people, and it implies a certain degree of formality which inappropriate in this context; it is not as if the *mass hysteria* was court-ordered. *To languish* means *to fade* or *to lose vigor* and is the opposite of what we are looking for. The correct answer is *fester* (*to rot* or *to rankle*)

109. *paradox* and *bombastic*

This passage implies that Cyrano is of a somewhat contradictory nature; he *swaggers*, which suggests arrogance, but he is also *insecure*. Keep this in mind when filling in the first blank. An *archetype* is *an original model from which all things of the same kind are copied*. This passage does not discuss the effects of *Cyrano de Bergerac* on future literature, so you can eliminate this choice. *Cliche* is too negative a word for this passage, which is generally appreciative of the play; it means *a trite or hackneyed plot, character development, use of color, etc*. The correct answer is *paradox*, which means *any person, thing, or situation exhibiting an apparently contradictory nature*.

To fill in the second blank, we are looking for an adjective that can modify *words* and, probably, relate in some way to *swagger*. *Licentious* means *lewd* or *immoral* - something that this passage nowhere implies Cyrano to be. Eliminate it. *Iconoclastic* (*attacking or ignoring cherished beliefs and long-held traditions*) is slightly more plausible if you know anything about the play being discussed, but we still have no reason to believe, based on this passage that someone who is arrogant is also a revolutionary. This leaves you with *bombastic*, which means *high-flown* or *pompous*, and is often used to describe speech.

110. *manifest, incumbent upon* and *abysmal*

If people were surprised by this man's decision to teach, he must have had at least a passing interest in performing, so look for a word that reflects this. *Inordinate* (*not within proper or reasonable limits*) is too strong, given that it implies his interest was excessive and unhealthy. If his interest were merely *perfunctory*, however, it is unlikely anyone would be surprised; it means *hasty and superficial* or *indifferent*. *Manifest* (*evident* or *obvious*) is the correct answer.

Given that he decided to teach in spite of this, he must have felt it was important in some way - keep this in mind when filling in the second blank. *Inimical to* is certainly not the correct answer; he would surely no choose to do something that was *harmful* or *hostile* to him. On the other hand, he would have to have a fairly high opinion of himself to say that his decision was *munificent of* (*very generous of*) him. The correct answer is *incumbent upon* (*obligatory*).

As for the last blank, try to think of why he might feel obligated to teach - presumably because he feels that the *state of arts education in the public schools* needs improving. To say that arts education is *banal*, however, would be a bit harsh; the purpose of elementary and secondary arts programs isn't really innovation, so it would be unfair to criticize them as *hackneyed* or *trite*. *Odious* is also too strong a word, though for different reasons. It means *hateful* or *detestable,* which implies some degree of moral condemnation. The best answer is *abysmal,* which means *extremely bad or severe.*

111. *indiscernible* and *brazen*

     Casual listeners are presumably not as attuned as researchers to the differences in question, so look for a word that means something like *unnoticeable. Pertinent* means *relevant,* which won't work in this context; the differences are presumably *relevant* to people other than *casual listeners* or the study would not have taken place. *Blatant (flagrant* or *conspicuous)* is the opposite of what we are looking for. The correct answer is *indiscernible (imperceptible).*

     Where the second blank is concerned, we know from the word *condemn* that we are looking for a word with negative connotations that could describe a *romantically assertive* woman. *Garish* is not quite what we want; it means *crudely or tastelessly colorful, showy* or *excessively ornate,* and is not usually used to describe people. *Capricious,* on the other hand, is not quite negative enough for this context; it means *erratic* or *flighty,* which are not strong enough criticisms to warrant *condemnation. Brazen (shameless* or *impudent)* is a better answer.

112. *aegis*

     We are told that 3M is *diversified* and does business in a variety of different areas; clearly the sentence means to say that all of these branches fall under the *control* or *supervision* of 3M. *Vagaries* does not make sense; if all of its divisions were subject to its *unpredictable or erratic actions,* the business would probably not be successful. *Covenant* is more often used in a religious context; it means a *formal agreement.* An *opus* is a *composition* - either literary or musical - and is clearly irrelevant to this passage. *Tutelage,* on the other hand, implies that the different branches of 3M are more like apprentice companies; it means *instruction* or *guidance.* The best answer is *aegis (protection* or *support).*

113. *reaches, fathom* and *velocities and trajectories*

     The best answer for the first blank is *reaches. Reaches* suggests both the immensity and sense of the unknown that the rest of entry describes.

     The best answer for the second blank is *fathom.* The rest of the entry is not concerned with measuring or explaining the universe, only imagining its immensity.

     The best answer for the third blank is *velocities and trajectories.* This answer is the only one that refers to directional movement.

114. *contend, coterie* and *cohesive style*

     The best answer for the first blank is *contend.* This answer best reflects that there is a debate among scholars.

     The best answer for the second blank is *coterie.* A *coterie* is a *group of people,* whereas a *menagerie* is a *group of animals; gild* would be a possible answer, but *gild* here means *to coat in gold.*

     The best answer for the third blank is *cohesive style.* The entry refers to a seamless collaboration between writers as a style, rather than a particular tone within the writing.

115. sequence, *assistance* and *less coordination*

     The best answer for the first blank is *sequence.* The sentence indicates there are several gears to be shifted through, as in a *sequence.*

     The best answer for the second blank is *assistance.* The entry must reflect the lack of action required from the driver.

     The best answer for the third blank is *less coordination.* That a driver must shift a manual but do nothing in an automatic suggests less coordination is needed in an automatic.

116.   *lithe* and *associate*

The best answer for the first blank is *lithe*. The entry must be synonymous with the moves of a dancer, which are known to be *graceful*.

The best answer for the second blank is *associate*. The two things, *gazelles* and *dancers*, are being compared as similar to one another.

117.   *acumen* and *learned*

The best answer to the first blank is *acumen*. This answer best refers to the education needed *to run a business*. The best answer to the second blank is *learned*. This also best relates back to the need for education in a particular area to run a business.

118.   *ore* and *composites*

The best answer for the first blank is *ore*. *Unrefined and buried metals* are best known as *ore*, whereas *magma* is *molten rock*.

The best answer for the second blank is *composites*. This entry indicates the combining of refined metals, whereas the others refer to the ore as it exists in the ground.

119.   *cognizant*

The best answer is *cognizant*. The entry must refer to awareness, and no other choice fits.

120.   *precarious* and *origin*

The best answer for the first blank is *precarious*. Although not a perfect answer, it best refers to the dangers of the long journey of a butterfly.

The best answer for the second blank is *origin*. The entry is concerned with location and travel distances.

121.   *localized*

The best answer is *localized*. The subject is the location of the squirrels, rather than type, as the beginning of the sentence may suggest.

122.   *hurtle* and *extirpated*

The best answer for the first blank is *hurtle*. The entry refers to fast, explosive movement, so this answer is better than *waft*.

The best answer for the second blank is *extirpated*. A meteor that is *extirpated* has completely disintegrated in the atmosphere, leaving nothing to fall to Earth.

123.   *rancor* and *moribund*

The second sentence indicates that the reforms have been stalled *indefinitely*; in other words, they are *moribund*, the best choice for the second blank.

Given the *repressive* nature of the government and the status of the *reforms*, the best choice for the first blank is *rancor*, since it is more likely, in the context, that the people will resent the government than be loyal or disgusted.

124.   *cupidity* and *surfeit*

The best choice for the first blank is *cupidity* since the sentence implies that the dictator had an excessive lust for material goods.

The clause following the dash indicates that the dictator had acquired an *overabundance*, or *surfeit* of material possessions.

125. *probity*

The best choice to fill in the blank is probity, since the passage indicates that the judge is upstanding and has considerable integrity.

126. *assiduously*

The best choice is assiduously. The sentence suggests that the group put consistent time and effort into the project - in other words, they worked assiduously.

127. *effrontery*

The passage suggests that the waiter was rude and presumptuous, so the best choice for the blank is effrontery.

128. *loquacious*

The best choice is loquacious. Although the seat mate being irascible or rapacious could explain why the writer was unable to read or sleep, the most logical choice in context is that he was very talkative, or loquacious.

129. *espousing* and *grandiose*

The best choice for the first blank is espousing. The second sentence points to an instance of a European ruler adopting, or espousing ties to ancient Rome.

The best choice for the second blank is grandiose, since it is the only choice that makes sense in context.

130. *lucid*

The passage indicates that Walt's presentation had the effect of making some previously unclear goals more accessible. Thus, the best choice is lucid; Walt's presentation was clear.

Sentence Equivalence

1.   *forerunners and antecedents*

The blank needs to be filled by a word that refers to things that came before 1789; derivatives, descendents, and imitators can therefore be ruled out from the start. Originators could be used in the sentence, but is not equivalent to any of the other options, leaving antecedents and forerunners.

2.   *stimulated and motivated*

The negative dampened and debilitated do not belong in the sentence. Abetted fits well in the sentence, but emphasizes the notion that Einstein's work helped the work that followed, which may be true, but such a meaning is not equivalent to the meaning of any of the other options. Vitalize is what can happen to something already in existence. Since work based on Einstein's discovery did not exist until after the he had made the discovery, the discovery did not vitalize the work that came after it, instead the discovery stimulated or motivated the work that followed.

3.   *drawn and derived*

In the sentence, drawn and derived refer to a conclusion based on Newton's physics. The other options refer to actions and/or thought processes, none of which are equivalent to each other or to drawn or derived.

4.   *entails and involves*

In the sentence, entails and involves indicate that when one does chemical thermodynamics, one also does "measurements of thermodynamic properties and . . ." Subsumes means "take the place of," constitutes means "is the same as," embodies means represents, and contains would indicate that chemical thermodynamics is some sort of container for "measurements. . ."

5.   *motivated and influenced*

Motivated and influenced convey that the "young woman" was inspired by "her desire to impress her parents." Inhibited, sedated, and stymied suggest different levels of negative influence and do not fit well in the sentence. Adjudicated, has no other similar word among the options.

6.   *deductive* and *inferable*

This passage is saying that humans do not possess the capabilities, scientifically, to explicitly see the scientific truths that we want to see. Therefore we must rely on something to overcome our "empirical handicap." "Inverse" means to render in the opposite direction. This would not help us understand faraway truths because it would just make them equally distant in another capacity. "Deliberate" means slow and careful. This looks like a good answer at a glance but just because you work slowly at something you lack the scientific capability to do doesn't mean you'll ever get there. You're still terminally unequipped. "Observable" means capable of being seen. This misses the entire point the sentence is going for: these things *can't* be seen. You can't use "Observable" evidence to study something that is implied to be unobservable. "Obvious" means easy to ascertain. This answer is also wrong because the entire point of the sentence is that these Universal truths are *not* easy to ascertain. This leaves "Deductive" and "Inferable." Both of these words mean capable of being apprehended through inference. This is exactly what would be needed to overcome lack of direct observation: the ability to work backwards and reason the existence of a concept. Therefore, **c** and **d** are correct.

7.   *subverted* and *undermined*

This sentence is saying that modern superficial standards have damaged the media, and done something to children. If it damaged all of modern media then it can be safely assumed that it damaged children, too. "Initiated" means began. If superficiality initiated confidence then it would be helping children, so that answer must be wrong. "Rectified" means fixed. Again, since superficiality is described as doing damage then this answer cannot be correct. "Invigorated" means strengthened. Again, this sentiment is the opposite of what the sentence wants to convey. To invigorate confidence would be a good thing, "Objectified" means portrayed, often with negative connotations. But it is beauty that is being objectified, not the self-confidence of children. The self-confidence of children is collateral damage. Therefore, "Subverted" and "Undermined" are the correct answers. They both mean damaged or weakened. The modern superficiality is damaging the self-confidence of young children. This makes perfect sense. So, **a** and **b** are correct.

8.   *inconspicuous* and *subtle*

This sentence is saying that very different conditions can be misdiagnosed because there is "something" about the differences in their symptoms that cause them to be confused. This "something" must be a vagueness that renders them easily confused. "Pervasiveness" means prevalence. The amount of the symptoms wouldn't hinder a doctor's ability to differentiate between them. "Harmless" means non-threatening. The harmlessness of the differences wouldn't affect a doctor's ability to differentiate between symptoms, either. "Debilitating" means incapacitating. If the differences were debilitating it would actually make proper diagnosis easier because they would have such different effects on a patient. "Extravagant" means excessive. Again, excessive differences would make proper diagnosis easier. We want differences that are hard to notice. That leaves us with "Inconspicuous" and "Subtle." These both mean difficult to locate. Differences in symptoms that follow these two descriptions would, in fact, be difficult to spot and would lead to misdiagnosis. **a** and **e are correct.**

9.   *proficiency* and *expertise*

"Aggression" means violence or hostility. This doesn't work in the sentence because violence is not a characteristic a doctor must possess to perform a difficult surgery. "Reticence" means reserve or quietness. This answer also does not complete the sentiment of the sentence because it's already been established that the doctor is audacious. "Reticence" would contradict the word audacious. "Contempt" means disdain or scorn. There is no reason to believe that disdain or scorn would aid a doctor in completing a complicated surgical procedure. "Delusion" is misunderstanding. Again, misunderstanding the topic at hand would not help a doctor perform a surgery – it would hinder him or her. This leaves "Proficiency" and "Expertise." Both of these words mean aptitude or skill. A doctor would certainly need to compliment his or her daring with an equal amount of ability. Therefore, choices **c** and **f** are correct.

10.   *hounding* and *badgering*

If we read the sentence, we get the sensation that the person is annoyed by being asked repeatedly to fix a problem. The words hounding and badgering are the best options because both of these words mean to annoy or irritate repeatedly. The other word choices bearing, ferreting and weaseling have nothing to do with reminding a person to constantly do something. They are words that mean to move or in a certain way (bearing), to look for something persistently (ferreting), and to cheat somebody (weaseling). Remonstrating means to protest or object strongly to something and would not complete the sentence properly.

11.   *endemic* and *prevalent*

In the above sentence, we are led to believe that there is a lot of crime in the area and even the police are hesitant to go in after nightfall. The two words that would best complete the sentence would be endemic and prevalent. Epidemic refers to the wide spread of virus, curtailed means something has been lessened, governable would mean that the problem was controllable and exuberant means exciting, lively or happy - all of which would not complete the above sentence in a logical manner.

12.   *drifted* and *wafted*

The correct word option is one that means to come through. The correct word choices are drifted and wafted. The words coasted, transmitted, poised and inured make no sense when completing the above sentence. Coasted means to sail or slide by, transmitted means to emit a signal or information, poised means to be calm or balanced, and inured means to become an advantage or to make someone become accustomed to something disagreeable such as children to sex and violence.

13.   *twilight* and *crepuscular*

The keyword in the sentence above is evening. We are looking for words that refer to the evening, words such as twilight and crepuscular. Diurnal refers to the day time, noontide refers to 12 o'clock noon, enlightened means to become aware of and modicum is a tiny portion or a limited quantity.

14.   *pristine* and *immaculate*

In the above sentence, the words remarkable, condition and high standard all lead us to believe that the missing word describes how well the book has been preserved. Sanitary is used to describe how clean something is e.g. a hospital, untarnished is mainly used for metals or for describing a person's reputation, purified refers to something that has been through a purifying process and adulterated means something that has been manipulated or tampered with. The only two word choices left are pristine and immaculate. These two word choices refer to the excellent condition of a book that generally would not be, because of its age.

15.   *clumsy* and *gauche*

Clumsy and gauche are the only two word options possible because they are the only options that complete the sentence logically Clumsy and gauche in this sentence both mean crude or badly done. Sophisticated would not make any sense in the sentence since the designs were unpopular and unpractical. The word choice ill-bred refers to a person who is impolite while butterfingered is used to describe a person who is extremely clumsy and drops things. Lastly, couth is used to describe something or someone extremely sophisticated.

16.   *dilettante* and *amateur*

The key phrase in the sentence is in spite of. This phrase leads us to believe that there is a contrast in ideas and the missing word most likely means lack of knowledge or not being profuse in a subject. The word choices that would best fit this idea would be dilettante and amateur. The word unskilled refers to a person's skill and has nothing to do with knowledge, dabbling is the action of taking a superficial interest in something; connoisseur and proficient both mean being an expert or extremely knowledgeable on the topic.

17.   *profuse* and *plenteous*

The word choices that don't make sense in the sentence are barren, elaborate, pretentious and luxuriant. Barren means not being able to bear fruit, arid and dry, elaborate is usually not used to describe a person's hair unless we're describing their hairstyle, pretentious describes someone who makes claims of undeserved self-importance and, luxuriant is generally used with vegetation (or material riches) and means profuse or very fertile. It is generally not used with hair unless we're referring to hair growth. Therefore, the word options, profuse which means abundant and plenteous which means generous are the correct answers.

18.   *ornate* and *baroque*

Ornate and baroque are the best words to describe the marble columns. The rest of the words do not complete the sentence in a meaningful way. Clement is used to refer to mild weather, embroidered is something that has been sewn with a picture or design, dowdy means dull or boring and from the context of the sentence the columns are not dull or boring. Garish means loud and flashy which is also unlikely in a beautiful and elegantly designed 15th-century church.

19. *capacious* and *expansive*

Here, in the above sentence, the keywords are *despite* and *undersized*, and because *despite* is used when there is a contrast in ideas, we are looking for a word that would mean the opposite of *undersized*, a word that means spacious. Capacious and expansive would therefore be the most logical word choices. Abundance means a large quantity but cannot be used here because we must say 'abundance of' something, brimming is normally used when something exceeds its capacity as in a liquid; minute refers to something very small and the word discrepant means disagreeing and would not logically make sense in the sentence.

20. *contrived* and *devised*

In the above, the marketing team has done something to improve sales. We are looking for a word that means planned or came up with; therefore the best word options to complete the sentence logically would be contrived and devised. The word connived also means to come up with, however it has a negative connotation as does the word schemed; as a consequence neither word would complete the sentence in a meaningful way. Blueprints are plans or designs drawn up by architects and casted means to throw or to make an impression of.

21. *fraudulent* and *dubious*

Here, the main idea is that something is being done by firms, something to inflate their profits and something that is misleading or dishonest. The best options to replace the missing word would be fraudulent and dubious. Counterfeit means an imitation. In this sentence, it cannot be used because you cannot make a counterfeit accounting practice, although you can make counterfeit documents or money. Infamous means to be notorious and is generally used to describe people, villainess is a quality used to describe a person who acts like a villain or that is evil and, slanderous means to tell lies about a person to discredit him.

22. *frugal* and *parsimonious*

The keyword in the sentence is "recession". Companies are now doing something with their marketing budgets that they probably didn't use to do before the recession when markets were buoyant. We are looking for a word that means "to be careful with money". The most logical answers to complete the sentence would be frugal and parsimonious which both mean to be cautious with money. Miserly has a negative connotation and refers to being cheap or mean with money. Gluttonous means to be voracious, altruistic means to be generous and to give to good causes and lavish would mean to be extremely generous, all of which a company would not be inclined to do during times of financial difficulty.

23. *primitive* and *archaic*

While most of the word options mean, to some extent, something that is outdated or old, not all of them can be used in the above sentence. Old-fashioned and antiquated are used to describe something that is out of date, not fashionable or something that is not really used anymore. Obsolete is used for something that is no longer used or is useful. Trampled makes no sense because it means to walk over forcibly. The two options left are primitive and archaic, both refer to something ancient that is generally no longer in existence.

24. *controversial* and *polemic*

The key phrase here is child slavery; and a publication (book or news article) about such a topic that might cause some controversy. Hence the correct missing word options are controversial and polemic.

Quarrelsome means to cause a fight and while the topic is controversial; it is unlikely to cause fights. Metaphysical is a term meaning without physical presence and does not complete the sentence logically. Cantankerous is used to describe a person who is grumpy or bad humored.

25. *materialistic* and *bourgeois*

The best word choices to complete the sentence are materialistic and bourgeois. The two words socialists and capitalist are keywords because they help determine the missing word. Socialists disapprove of capitalists; they would not like excessive spending on material things. Socialists also disapprove of the rich or wealthy middle-class, i.e. the bourgeois. Knowing this allows us to choose materialistic and bourgeois as the correct word options. Nonconforming, indolent, Victorian and capitalism would not make any sense in the above sentence. Nonconforming has nothing to do with excesses, indolent means lazy, Victorian is an adjective that refers to Victorian England and capitalism is an ideology and not used as a word to describe excesses.

26. *indigenous* and *aboriginal*

The word missing from the above sentence is a synonym of the word native - as in native tribes. Indigenous and aboriginal are both words used to designate native peoples of a land. Homegrown is not possible because you cannot grow a tribe, nor is it likely you can inherit a tribe. It also would not make sense to gather genetic data from an alien tribe. The word inbred is not possible because it means the interbreeding or exchange of ideas within a culture or people.

27. *disparities* and *discrepancies*

The word options disparities and discrepancies are the best options to complete the sentence since the words refer to the economic difference between first and third world countries. While the word *hole* and *burrow* are synonyms for gap, they are not used in an economic sense. Animosity means hateful or spiteful while disagreeable means something that is not agreeable. Neither option would make sense when used in the above sentence.

28. *bilious* and *sallow*

The word options hearty, salubrious and vigorous are all synonyms of the word healthy, and if a person is ill, his/her complexion is not going to be healthy. Albino is a type of genetic condition and does not make sense in the sentence. The two possible answers would be bilious and sallow. Both words are adjectives used to describe a person who is not looking very healthy or well.

29. *profusion* and *accretion*

This question stem sets up a contrast; some residents are displaced while others enjoy the new additions to the community. The missing answer will support the idea of addition or growth in the community. Choice (B)-abridgement (meaning to shorten or condense) is the opposite of growth. Choice(C)-ardor (meaning great emotion or passion), Choice (D)-parapet (meaning fortification consisting of a low wall and, Choice(F)-culmination (meaning conclusion) are all off-topic for this sentence. The correct answers are Choice(A)profusion – meaning extreme abundance and Choice (E)-accretion (meaning a gradual increase in size, as through growth or external addition

30. *perspicacity* and *sagacity*

The Internet is providing a window or a look into other cultures; the missing word will provide a similar meaning to "a look" or "insight". Choice(B)-erudition and Choice(D)-sapience both mean intelligence which is the incorrect idea for this sentence. Choice (E)-apotheosis (meaning the epitome of perfection or the elevation to the status of a deity) and Choice (F)-proclivity (meaning tendency or inclination) are off-topic for the question stem. The correct answer choices are Choice (A)-perspicacity (meaning insight or understanding) and Choice (C)-sagacity (meaning insight and wisdom).

31. *bated* and *minified*

The sentence presents a change over time; Previously, household tasks took up substantial time, but the appliances have changed that tremendously Therefore, the correct answer will support the idea of the tasks being reduced. Choice(E)-impinged (meaning to infringe upon or advance beyond the normal limit) and Choice(F)-augmented (meaning making something greater in number or strength) are the opposite meanings needed for the missing word. Choice(C)-masticated (meaning to bite or grind with the teeth) and Choice(D)-attenuated (meaning reduced in strength)both mean reduced but with the wrong connotation to suit the question stem. The correct answers are Choice(A)-bated (meaning diminished) and Choice (B)-minified (meaning lessened).

32. *plethora* and *legion*

The question stem indicates that there are thousands of harmful organisms in the body. Without the immune system, these numerous organisms could attack the body. The correct answer will correspond with the idea of "numerous" or "thousands". Choice (B)-surfeit (meaning the state of being more than full), Choice (D)-consanguinity (meaning a close relation or connection, particularly a blood relationship), Choice (F)-extolment (meaning an expression of approval and commendation), and Choice (E)-peculation (meaning a fraudulent appropriation of funds entrusted in your care but owned by someone else)are all off-topic for this question stem. The correct answers are Choice (A)-plethora and Choice (C)-legion both of which mean a large number.

33. *fastidiously* and *punctiliously*

The microscope allows people to see something as small as an organism's cell easily; therefore we can deduce the correct answer will support the idea of seeing better or more clearly. None of the incorrect answers fit into the scope of the sentence; Choice(A)-mendaciously (meaning in an untruthful manner), Choice (B)-salubriously (meaning healthy to the mind or body), Choice (C)-adventitiously (meaning associated by chance and not integral) do not correspond with "in detail". Choice (F)-exiguously (meaning deficient in amount or quality or extent) also does not make sense in the sentence. The correct answers are Choice(D)-fastidiously and (E)punctiliously, which both mean painstakingly and carefully.

34. *tamable* and *tractable*

The message of the sentence is that scientists created a naming system to make identifying one animal for another more of something. Naming systems help to define and categorize things, so we can deduce these systems likely make identifying animals easier or more manageable. The missing word likely have a similar connotation to "simpler" or "manageable". Choice (B)-vociferous (meaning conspicuously and offensively loud), Choice (C)-resplendent (meaning having great beauty), Choice(D)-quiescent (meaning being quiet and still), and Choice(E)-glib (meaning slick or insincere speech) are all off-topic for this question stem. The correct answers are Choice (A)-tamable (meaning controllable) and Choice (F)-tractable (meaning easily managed).

35. *impart* and *bestow*

The question stem describes what the neutrons contribute to the nucleus; the neutrons contribute to the mass of the nucleus but do not contribute to the electric charge of the nucleus. The correct answer will align with the idea of contributing or transferring from one to another. Choice (A) extenuate (meaning to lessen the importance) and Choice (F) ossify (meaning to become hard and bony) are incorrect because they do not refer in any way to contributing. Choice (D) remit (meaning to give money) and Choice (E) bequeath (meaning to give possessions in the case of death) both mean to contribute in some way, but they are incorrect because they carry the wrong connotation for the sentence. The correct answers are (B) impart – meaning to transmit or pass on and (C) bestow – meaning to give or transfer an honor.

36.   *substantive* and *indispensable*

The question stem describes the nucleus as providing major functions for the atom. The missing word will reflect this – that the nucleus is a significant part of an atom. Choice(A)-effulgent (meaning brilliant or radiating) and Choice(E)recondite (meaning confined to and understandable by only an enlightened inner circle)do not fit the scope of the sentence. Choice (C)-epochal (meaning so significant that it brings about a new era), and Choice (F)-evidentiary (meaning important based on evidence) all refer to some aspect of the word "significant", but the connotation of each word is not fitting for the question stem. The correct answers are (B)substantive – meaning important or essential and (D)indispensable– meaning necessary or vital.

37.   *affiliated* and *colligated*

For this question, the missing word is defined in the sentence: metabolism is associated with more processes than just converting fat to energy. The correct answer will have a similar meaning to "associated". None of the incorrect answers support the idea of "associated"; Choice (C)-caviled (meaning to quibble or make unnecessary objections), Choice (D)-distended (meaning to swell, to inflate, to bloat), Choice (E)-ensconced (meaning to fix or settle firmly), and Choice (F)-abrogated (meaning to formally abolish) all do not fit within the scope of the sentence. The correct answers are Choice (A)-affiliated (meaning to associate) and Choice (B)-colligated (meaning to make a logical connection).

38.   *consideration* and *expatiation*

The key idea in this sentence "have determined"; by this we know meteorologists have studied or examined hurricane activity in order to draw conclusions about its timing. The missing word will correspond with the idea of an examination or the undertaking of a study. Choice (A)-cogitation (meaning deep thought), Choice (D)-introspection (meaning contemplation), and Choice(F)-rumination (also meaning contemplation) do relate to examining, but the connotation is not proper for this sentence. These three words refer to examining for the purpose of understanding and not examining for the purpose of analyzing. Choice (C)-circumlocution (meaning a lengthy, round-about expression) is off-topic for this sentence. The correct answers are Choice (B)-consideration (meaning the process of weighing carefully) and Choice (E)-expatiation (meaning a discussion that enlarges a topic).

39.   *homogenous* and *undifferentiated*

The message of the sentence is that there are many different types of governments in place around the world; in other words, the governments throughout the world are far from "the same". The correct answer will mean "the same". Choice(A)-bilious (meaning irritable or ill-tempered) and Choice(B)-lachrymose (meaning sorrowful) are incorrect as they do fit the scope of the sentence. Choice(E)-discrete (meaning separate) and Choice(F)-disjointed (meaning unconnected) have similar meanings, but they do not mean "the same". The correct answers are Choice(C)-homogenous (meaning of the same nature) and Choice-(D)undifferentiated (meaning the same kind or lacking diversity).

40.   *sequestered* and *insular*

Imperialism resulted in ethnic groups that were once unacquainted with each other now living in the same nation. The correct answer will reflect the first part of the story – that these nations were not in close contact. Choice(B)-parochial (meaning narrow-minded and restricted to new ideas) and Choice(E)-illiberal (meaning close-minded and intolerant) both mean restricted, but they are incorrect because they refer to the restriction of opinions rather than of any physical space. Choice (C)-sectarian (meaning a subgroup of a larger group) and Choice(F)-catholic (meaning including a wide variety of things or all-embracing) are the opposite of the idea or groups not in close contact. The correct answers are Choice(A)-sequestered (meaning secluded from others) and Choice(C)-insular (meaning isolated).

41.   *quell* and *obviate*

The founding fathers are attempting find solutions to disagreements, or in other words, suppressing or eliminating conflict. The correct answer will have a similar meaning to "suppressing" or "eliminating". Choice (D)-exacerbate (meaning to increase bitterness or violence), and Choice (F)-precipitate (meaning to hasten or bring about) are incorrect; they are both the opposite of the needed meaning. Choice(B)-castigate (meaning to criticize harshly) and Choice (C)-emulate (meaning to strive to equal or excel) do not fit the scope of the sentence. The correct answers are Choice(A)-quell (meaning to stamp out) and Choice (E)-obviate (meaning to do away with).

42.   *intransigent* and *recalcitrant*

In this sentence, having a criminal record prevents someone from taking part in basic social functions. The correct answers will support the idea of a criminal record as a significant obstacle. None of the incorrect answers all do not support the idea of a criminal record as a hard-to-get-around obstacle. : Choice(A)-culpable (meaning deserving blame or censure), Choice(B)-dogmatic (meaning pertaining to a code of beliefs), Choice(D)-emollient (meaning softening to the skin), Choice (F)-florid (meaning flush with a rosy color) The correct answers are Choice(C)-intransigent (meaning entrenched) and Choice(E)-recalcitrant (meaning stubbornly resistant).

43.   *inextirpable* and *indelible*

The sentence lists many components of culture but highlights that a powerful component is a type of bond members feel. A bond is a connection that fastens things together, so the correct answer will support the idea of a strong or powerful tie. None of the incorrect answers support this idea: Choice(A)-irascible (meaning grouchy or cranky), Choice(B)-execrable (meaning abominable and utterly despicable), Choice (D)illustrious-(meaning famous or prominent), and Choice(E)-opprobious (meaning offensive and disgraceful). The correct answers are Choice(C)-inextirpable (meaning indestructible or unable to erase) and Choice(F)-indelible (meaning permanent and lasting).

44.   *innocuous* and *aberrant*

The message of the sentence is that the media can be used in multiple ways; some people use media in one way while others use media in another way. One way is disruptive to society, but the other way - the contrast to disruptive - is exemplified by fashion and hairstyle trends. Choice (C)-injurious (meaning to cause harm) is incorrect; this word provides a similar idea to disruptive or destructive, and we need a word that means the opposite. Choice(E)-equivocal (meaning doubtful or uncertain) is incorrect as the sentence describes very certain ways the media influences others. Choice(B)-aberrant (meaning deviating from the normal) and Choice(E)-exorbitant (meaning exceeding or outside of customary limits) do not fit the scope of the sentence; using media to forward fashion trends is actually quite normal. The correct answers are (A)innocuous – meaning harmless and (B) banal – meaning commonplace, ordinary, or usual. These two words do not have exactly the same meaning, but both of them fit into the sentence in a way that makes sense overall.

45.   *erudite* and *lofty*

The liberal arts education is now seen as an area of study not practical for today's society. The correct answer must evoke the opposite of "practical" and "down-to-earth". Choice (C)-asinine (meaning lacking intelligence or foolish) and Choice (D)-obtuse (meaning not quick or alert in perception, feeling, or intellect) both relate to learning, but both are incorrect because neither provides a contrast with "practical". Choice(F)-fetid (meaning foul-smelling, putrid, stinking) is not relevant to this question stem. Choice(E)-chary (meaning cautiously or suspiciously reluctant to do something) does not fit in this sentence; no indication is given that anyone dedicating years of study to liberal arts should be cautious or suspicious).The correct answers are (A)erudite – meaning scholarly and (B) lofty – meaning high-minded both provide a direct contrast with the idea of a practical, down-to-earth education.

46. *encountered* and *happened upon*

    Affronted, emulated, and *studied*, would indicate that the corporations took various specific actions in response to the problems. *Took on* would suggest the likely scenario that the corporations learned about the problems and took steps to solve them. The correct options, *encountered* and *happened upon*, have no similar words among the options and indicate only that the corporations came into contact with problems, not that they did anything in response to these problems.

47. *casual* and *dispassionate*

    The pairs *casual/dispassionate* and *curious/interested* fit in the sentence, but the correct options agree with the context of the sentence because the fact that a watch increases in mass when wound would not be necessarily surprising to someone who was thinking (i.e. *curious* and *interested*) about the issue. *Heedless* is similar in meaning to *casual* and *dispassionate* but has a negative sense not entailed in the correct options. Similarly, *concerned* is similar to *curious* and *interested*.

48. *Inconceivable* and *implausible*

    Inconceivable and *implausible* indicate that the concept or idea at issue would not be possible. All *inconceivable* and implausible ideas are also questionable, but since not all questionable ideas are not inconceivable and implausible, *questionable* cannot be a correct choice *Cogitable* would mean that evolution could be imaginable, and *incontestable* and *probable* are positive terms where the sentence requires negative words such as *inconceivable* and *implausible* Also, none of the incorrect options mean the same as any of the other options.

49. *effectiveness* and *productivity*

    While all the options fit will in the blank, only *effectiveness* and *productivity* refer in the sentence to the same *concept* and so all other options are incorrect.

50. *apprehensive* and *uneasy*

    Boorish, unassertive, and *worrisome* can be ruled out because they have to do with different ways of *interacting* with others. Unfazed would mean that the *white males* in question are not bothered by company policy, a meaning at odds with the sense of the sentence. The remaining options, *apprehensive* and *uneasy*, are similar in meaning and fit well in the sentence.

51. *sensible and* sensitive

    Sensitive and *sensible* imply only that the cells easily detect changes in their environment. The other terms *suggest* varying types of reaction to changes in the environment.

52. *advantage* and *edge*

    Ability can be rejected because the sense of the sentence conveys the idea that *ability* is not what the company risks losing. Dominance, *stranglehold*, and *superiority* would suggest that being distinctive *necessarily* leads to controlling the market, when in fact distinctiveness merely provides a competitive *edge* or *advantage*.

53. *indispensable* and *vital*

    The difference between the correct options and the other choices is that the wrong choices suggest that while the employee may be important to the company, if the company had hired someone else, that person would be just as important. Using your own creativity is contributing something that only you can provide, making you feel *vital* and *indispensable*.

54. *notable* and *remarkable*

    The *sentence* presents Bruegel's work in a positive light and thus *glaring* and *tawdry* do not fit in the sentence. *Eye-catching* has no synonym. *Famous* could be used as a synonym for either *remarkable* or *notable*, but *remarkable* and *notable* do not necessarily include the notion of fame, indicating only that vivid colors and realistic representations are an important dimension of the artist's work, whether he be *famous* or not.

55.   *infamous and notorious*

Notorious, *infamous*, and *ignominious* could be used as synonyms, but *ignominious* suggests insignificance, unlike the first two terms which suggest a degree of fame. *Famous* could be used because something *infamous* is also famous, but infamous and notorious entail a touch of negativity not present in the more neutral famous. *Great* and *preeminent* could also be used as synonyms, but they contradict the sense of the sentence.

56.   *aspersed* and *traduced*

Exculpated must be rejected because it is a positive term where all the others are negative. *Disgraced*, *degraded*, and *repudiated* imply different meaning and none carry the notion, as do traduced and *aspersed*, *that* untrue things where said about the individual and music.

57.   *discriminative* and *perceptive*

All the terms would fit in the sentence and be true. The correct options fit best in the sentence because they center in on the specific trait needed to discern the sarcasm, while the other terms are more general.

58.   *eminent and salient*

Salient and *eminent* refer to a particular status gained by the *individual voice*, the other terms, except for *visible*, suggest that the *voice* is worth listening to, but do not necessarily imply that anyone actually is listening. *Visible* suggests, similar to the correct options, that people can hear the *voice* but does not imply that anyone is listening.

59.   *effectuating* and *observing*

The *options* relate closely to each other, but only the correct options convey the idea of putting into practice the basic property right. The other options refer to things that can be done *about* the right.

60.   *drafted* and *framed*

The correct options refer to charting a course. *Organized* and *prepared* suggest a degree of control over the coming *course* of action not supported by the rest of the sentence. *Calculated* and *schemed* also do not fit the sense of the sentence.

61.   *oppugnant* and *opprobrious*

The correct options mean offensive. *Disreputable* and *famous* agree with the sense of the sentence, but *famous conveys* that there may have been something positive about the letter, while *disreputable* is a negative term. *Shoddy* and *vicious* have no synonyms among the options.

62.   *manifested* and *revealed*

Projected and *publicized* would suggest that the information obtained became widely available and well known. *Uncloaked* and *unveiled* suggest that the information had been concealed. The correct options, agreeing with the sense of the sentence, indicate only that the information was discovered.

63.   *gamey* and *ribald*

Puckish, *impish*, and *ebullient* suggest that the plot was lively, but a lively plot would seem unlikely to offend *anyone*. *Phlegmatic* has no synonyms among the options, leaving *ribald* and *gamey* which suggest that the play had some potentially obscene content which would seem likely to offend.

64. *ascendance* and *hegemony*

   The incorrect options refer to specific types/levels of control not necessarily entailed in the generalized terms *ascendance* and *hegemony*. *Clout* refers to the influence over people, but is not usually used in reference to influence over products. *Privileges* is vague compared to the correct options, and *management* and *reign* refer to more specific types of influence than *ascendance* and *hegemony*.

65. *preponderant* and *sovereign*

   The correct options convey that Beethoven exerted an overwhelming influence on his successors. *Distinguished* and notable do not agree with towering, and *ancillary* and *auxiliary* suggest a weaker degree of influence than conveyed by the rest of the sentence.

66. *superintendence* and *sway*

   The correct options convey the notion of a controlling or leading influence. *Clout, privilege, importance,* and *place* can be used interchangeably in the sentence, as they suggest a degree of influence, but do not indicate a controlling or leading influence.

67. *co-optive* and *exploitive*

   Exploitive and *co-optive* convey the idea of the oppression of the weak by the strong and so fit better than the other words. *Deceptive* and *deleterious* have no synonyms among the options. The synonyms *benignant* and *beneficial* do not agree with the sense of the sentence.

68. *argosy* and *cornucopia*

   Argosy and *cornucopia* suggest a treasure trove of objects, while the other terms are more neutral. *Wellspring, while* more positive than the other wrong choices, would incorrectly suggest that the group of Picasso's work was replenishable.

69. chided *and excoriated*

   The near synonyms *exculpated* and *sanctioned* are positive terms that do not agree with the sentence. The correct options agree with the objective tone of the sentence and thus fit better than *libeled* and *slandered*.

70. *addled and graveled*

   The correct options refer to being confused by something. *Deluded* and *cozened* refer to being misled by something, a meaning not in accord with the rest of the sentence. *Agitated* and *stunned* refer to emotional states not necessarily in agreement with each other.

71. *standing* and *status*

   The correct options convey that the hypothesis will be useful to science if it is testable. *Position* and *rank* refer to places *on* a continuum rather than the on-or-off sense of *status* and *standing*. *Capacity* and *condition* have no synonyms among the options.

72. *credit* and *stock*

   Credit and *stock* convey the idea of faith or trust. *Force* is close to *stock* but *credit* is closer. *Dubiety* and *progeny have* no synonyms among the options.

73. *conditioned* and *primed*

   The correct *options* convey the notion that events in one country are influenced by those in another. The synonyms *habituated* and *inured* do not agree with the sense of the sentence and *recast* and *accommodated* have no synonyms among the options.

74.   *universals* and *generality*

The *phrase that living things have in common* requires the options *universals* and *generality*. The synonyms *specifics* and *details* do not go well with *have in common* nor do *circumscription* and *precision*.

75.   *eerie and uncanny*

Eerie and *uncanny* agree with the overall tone of the sentence and especially the word *frightened*. *Interesting* and *striking* on the one hand, and *curious* and *surprising*, on the other, suggest a more neutral emotional response not in keeping with the sentence.

76.   *means* and *mechanism*

The *correct* options are the only synonyms in the list. Do not be misled by median vs. medium.

77.   *novel* and *original*

While *innovative* and *ingenious* fit fairly well in the sentence, *novel* and *original* fit better because the *emphasis* of the sentence is on new discoveries, not on whether the discoveries are *innovative* or *ingenious*. *Germinal* and *primal* have to do with the beginnings of things, and do not fit well in the sentence.

78.   *dissemination* and *propagation*

Dissemination and *propagation* refer to a purposeful spreading of ideas, while *dispersal* and *dissipation* refer to *random* scattering. *Collection* and *concentration* do not work as synonyms in the sentence.

79.   *evinced and substantiated*

The *correct* options indicate that Pasteur showed that spontaneous generation could not occur. *Divulged* and *publicized* don't fit well with *definitively*, and *adduced* and *disconfirmed* have no synonyms in the options.

80.   *significance* and *worth*

Preeminence, prominence, and *renown* refer to the visibility of something and *substantiveness* refers to the reality *of* something. Since the sentence indicates that in the 1860's, Mendel's work was important, but not famous, that is, not preeminent, prominent or renowned; the correct options are the best choices.

81.   *Nebulous* and *Dubious*

It is clear from the sentence structure that the missing word is meant to contrast with the second half of the sentence; we are told that *concrete business plans* lead to success, and we are looking for something that will *do you little good*. If you know the meanings of the answer choice, you should be able to eliminate a few of *them* relying solely on common sense. *Sagacious means wise*, and surely wise dreams stand a good chance of becoming a reality. *Cogent* means *convincing* and is usually used to describe arguments. Your best clue, however, is the use of the word *concrete* - whatever answers we pick must mean something like *hazy* or *indistinct*. *Craven* means *cowardly*, and *fervid* means *ardent* or *intense* - eliminate them. This leaves you with *nebulous* and *dubious*, which mean *indistinct* and *questionable*, respectively.

82.   *morbid* and *saturnine*

This sentence focuses on the kind of writing Poe is known for; *horror, mystery,* and *crumbling mansions* are all fairly dark words, so the description probably means something like *frightening* or *grim*. Even if you are unsure *of* their exact meanings, you might now that *whimsical* and *droll* have positive connotations, and can therefore eliminate them. *Esoteric* describes something that appeals to a very narrow range of people - not something that is a *perennial favorite* - so you can eliminate it. *Sublime* means *elevated* or *lofty*, and while it is not inconceivable that an author's work might be described as *sublime, ask* yourself if the word really has anything to do with the rest of the sentence - it doesn't. The correct answers are *morbid* and *saturnine*, which mean *gruesome* and *gloomy*.

83.   *dogged and indefatigable*

The gist of this sentence seems to be that Shackleton overcame many obstacles in order to keep his team safe, so the answer probably has to do with perseverance. *Desultory* means *inconsistent* - almost the opposite of what we need. *Phlegmatic* means *apathetic* or *sluggish* - another quality that would do a person little good in an emergency. *Erudite* and *preternatural* mean *learned* and *extraordinary* or *unnatural*. Neither of these has very much to do with the rest of the sentence, but if you are tempted to answer *preternatural*, check to see if there is another word with a similar meaning (there isn't). You are left with *dogged* and *indefatigable*, which mean *persistent or tenacious* and *untiring*.

84.   *clandestine* and *illicit*

If you don't know the story of King Arthur, you should at least be able to gather from the sentence that Lancelot and Guinevere's relationship is adulterous and that it must have been a secret at one point if Mordred is able to *expose* it. Look at the answer choices and see if there is a word that might make sense in the context of the sentence. *Noisome* means *offensive* or *noxious* and usually describes a smell; there is no evidence *suggesting* that the writer of the sentence has such a strongly negative opinion on the subject, but even if you were tempted to pick this as your answer, the fact that there are no near-synonyms for it among the other answers should dissuade you. Do not confuse *discrete* with *discreet* - *discrete* means *discontinuous* or *distinct* and doesn't make sense in this context. *Inchoate* means *rudimentary* and, again, does not have much to do with the rest of the sentence. *Gauche* means something like *tactless*; this should strike you as an understatement in the context of the sentence, but if it doesn't, you will probably realize that the other remaining answers - *illicit* and *clandestine* - have much more similar meanings and are a better fit.

85.   *portent and harbinger*

If scientists *concerned about climate change* find extreme weather *alarming*, they probably see it as an early effect of climate change, so the missing word must mean something like *preview* or *sign*. If the current bad weather were the *antithesis* of what is to come, there would be little reason for alarm, because *antithesis* means *the direct opposite*. *Vagary* means *an unpredictable event or action*. It is often pluralized, but if you don't know this, use common sense; scientists think the current weather *is* part of a predictable process. *Enigma* and *imbroglio* mean *a puzzle* and *a misunderstanding or confusing situation*, neither of which is relevant in this context. This leaves you with *portent* and *harbinger*, which both mean *omen*.

86.   *gregarious and extroverted*

Notice that the sentence is discussing the social behaviors of chimpanzees; you have probably seen *indigenous* used to describe animals, but it means *native to a particular region* and has nothing to do with the rest of the sentence. The sentence tells us that chimpanzees live in large groups and interact with each other, so the answer probably has something to do with how sociable they are. *Ascetic*, which means *austere*, clearly does not work. *Peripatetic* means *wandering* or *itinerant*; the sentence says nothing about the movements of chimpanzees, so you can eliminate it. *Redoubtable* means *formidable* or *fearsome* and, again, does not have much to do with the sentence as a whole. *Gregarious* and *extroverted*, however, both mean something like *sociable*, and are therefore the correct answers.

87.   *equivocated* and *prevaricated*

The sentence gives us reason to believe that the suspect is not being truthful; he *spins* a story but does not back it up with evidence. The missing word probably has to do with dishonesty. Although you might associate *suspects* with transgressing, do not be taken in; this particular sentence has nothing to do with the suspect breaking a law. You might also think a suspect would *fawn* - that is, act in a servile manner - towards his interrogators, but the sentence is not about this, and you can eliminate it. *To palpitate* means *to flutter or beat rapidly* and often describes a heartbeat. *To quaff* means *to drink deeply*. This leaves you with *equivocated* and *prevaricated*, which have very similar meanings; both have to do with speaking ambiguously or hedging in order to hide the truth.

88.   *latent* and *quiescent*

If the disease may never become *active*, the missing word must mean something like *inactive*. Do not be fooled into thinking *restive* means *at rest*; its real meaning is *restless*, and is nearly the opposite of what you want. *Inimical* means *harmful*, which diseases certainly are, but it doesn't describe a disease that is currently inactive. *Fulsome* means *offensive* or *disgusting* - eliminate it. *Discreet* means *prudent* and is used to describe people or their actions and behavior. This leaves you with *latent* and *quiescent* - the former means *present but not visible* and the latter means *quiet* or *inactive*.

89.   *flouted* and *spurned*

If women who had children out of wedlock were treated as outcasts, their actions were most likely seen as a violation of conventional social standards, so the missing word should mean something like *ignored* or *broke with*. *To condone* means *to pardon or approve* - nearly the opposite of what we want. *To extol* can be eliminated for similar reasons; it means *to praise*. *Wafted* and *Disinterred* have little to do with the sentence; the former means *to carry lightly* or *to float*, and the latter means *to exhume or unearth*. *Flouted* and *spurned* are the correct choices; both have to do with ignoring or rejecting something.

90.   *repudiate* and *abjure*

You have probably already heard of Galileo's appearance before the Inquisition, but if you haven't, this sentence informs you that he got into trouble with the Church for claiming that the sun was the center of the solar system. Clearly the *Church leaders* mentioned in the sentence did not approve of his beliefs. This should help you to rule out *beatify*; the Church would hardly have *officially blessed* Galileo's ideas. *Foment* means *to foster* or *to stir up*, and because the Church was interested in squashing Galileo's beliefs, not encouraging them, you can eliminate this. *Preclude* means *to prevent*, and *accrue* means *to accumulate* - eliminate them. The correct answers are *repudiate* and *abjure*, which mean *to renounce* or *to reject*.

91.   *shrewd* and *adroit*

The sentence suggests that while small businesses can get tax breaks, it may require a bit more effort, because they lack the resources available to larger companies. Their *management* probably needs to be skillful and determined, and we want a word that reflects this. *Meretricious* definitely does not work; it means *showy* or *based on pretense*, and we need a word that describes genuinely skillful management. *Dogmatic* means *stubborn* or *dictatorial*, and implies an arbitrary adherence to a set of rules (*dogma*); it has a negative connotation, and we are looking for a positive word. *Supine* and *ineluctable* simply are not relevant to the sentence; the former means *lying on one's back* and the latter means *certain or inescapable*. *Shrewd* (*astute*) and *adroit* (*skillful*) are the best answers.

92.   *castigated* and *upbraided*

Most mothers would be upset to learn that their child has been stealing, so the correct answer likely reflects displeasure - *scolded*, perhaps, or something similar to it. *To placate* means *to pacify or appease*; a son caught stealing might try to placate his mother, but the mother probably has little interest in calming her son down. You may confuse *descry* with *decry*, but the former actually means *to discern or see*, which has nothing to do with the rest of the sentence - eliminate it. The son might be *flustered* (*upset* or *confused*) by his mother's criticism, but her primary goal is probably not to upset him but rather to teach him a lesson, so you can eliminate this answer. *To vilify* means *to disparage* or *to speak ill of*; it is a strong word, and it is hard to imagine a mother doing this to her son, no matter how upset she is. This leaves you with *castigated* and *upbraided*, which both mean *scolded* or *reprimanded*.

93.   *fetid* and *noisome*

As the sentence itself states, a plant named after a corpse probably has a fairly bad odor. You might be tempted to pick *florid* simply because it looks as if it has something to do with flowers (which it does - think *floral*), but it means *ruddy* or *ornate*, neither of which works particularly well as a description of an odor. *Effete* and *pusillanimous* both have negative connotations, but neither fits into this sentence; the former means *worn out* or *degenerate*, and the latter means *cowardly*. *Hirsute* means *hairy* and is similarly out of place in this context. You are left with *fetid* and *noisome*, which are both commonly used to refer to offensive odors.

94.   *temerity* and *mettle*

For most peasants, the thought of saying anything at all to the Dauphin was probably somewhat daunting, so Joan of Arc must have had great self-confidence and/or courage to make such an enormous demand. *Temperance* means *self-restraint* and *recreancy* means *cowardice*. Neither of these would have gotten her very far, so you can eliminate them. *Fecklessness* means *ineffectiveness* or *laziness* and can be eliminated for similar reasons. *Paean* is wholly unrelated to the sentence; it refers to a song of joy or praise. The correct answers are *temerity* and *mettle*; the former means *boldness* (with a hint of recklessness or audacity) and the latter means *courage*.

95.   *benign* and *propitious*

If you are unfamiliar with the Gulf Stream, use common sense; a warm current probably moderates what would otherwise be a cold climate (it is *northern* Europe, after all). Given this, you should be able to eliminate most of the answer choices. *Provident* means *having foresight* - not a quality we generally associate with weather of any kind. *Aseptic* is similarly out of place in this context; it means *sterile* or *free from germs*. It makes little sense as a description of weather - eliminate it. *Inveterate* means *firmly established by long continuance* and is more commonly used to describe feelings or beliefs. *Torpid* means *sluggish* and has negative connotations; it is not inconceivable that someone might describe weather this way - say, during a hot and humid summer - but before you pick it, check to make sure there are no better answers. *Benign* and *propitious*, which mean *pleasant* and *favorable*, are more in line with the probable meaning of the sentence, and are therefore the best answers.

96.   *mellifluous* and *dulcet*

This sentence establishes a contrast between the *strident* sound of bagpipes and the sound of other instruments, so the missing word probably means *gentle* or *smooth*. *Stentorian* is commonly used to describe sounds, but it means *loud* or *resounding*, so you can eliminate it. *Lithe* means *supple* or *limber* and more commonly refers to bodies or other physical objects. *Obstreperous* means *unruly* or *boisterous* - almost the opposite of what we are looking for. *Abstruse* means *hard to understand* or *esoteric*, and makes no sense in this context; the author nowhere mentions whether certain instruments are more intellectually challenging than others. The correct answers are *mellifluous* and *dulcet*, which mean *sweetly flowing* and *melodious*.

97.   *quail* and *cower*

As we all know, and as the sentence tells us, many children are afraid of thunder, so we are looking for a verb that expresses that fear. *To rebuff* generally requires an object, and in any case has little to do with this sentence; it means *to reject or snub*. You can eliminate *clinch*, which means *to settle something decisively*, for similar reasons; it is generally used when a question or issue has been resolved, which is not the case in this sentence. *To demur* means *to take exception* or *to object*, and again, does not make sense in this context. Only by a great stretch of the imagination are the children *objecting* to anything here, so you should eliminate this answer. *To simper* means *to smile in a silly way* or *to smirk*; it has a negative connotation that the context here does not warrant. Moreover, people who are frightened usually do not smile in any manner at all. You are left with *quail* (*to lose heart or courage*) and *cower* (*to recoil or flinch*).

98.   *proscriptions* and *prohibitions*

In this question, we are looking for something that could *prevent* people from following their natural instincts - laws or rules, perhaps. *Idyll* can refer either to a kind of pastoral poem or to a pleasant event or episode, neither of which seems likely to dissuade people from anything. A *cabal* is a group of conspirators. It has a fairly specific meaning, and does not fit into this sentence; how often do you hear about the *cabals of* society? The phrase itself makes little sense, given that cabals are secretive rather than sanctioned by society. Eliminate this answer. A society prone to *vacillations* (*states of indecision* or *fluctuations*) would almost certainly be unable to exercise the kind of control Hobbes seems to have in mind, so you can eliminate this answer as well. *Dereliction* is wrong for similar reasons; it means *neglect* (as in *dereliction of duty*) and again, could hardly act as a deterrent. The correct answers are *proscriptions* and *prohibitions*, which both refer to a formal ban on something.

99.   *connoisseur* and *epicure*

The missing word in this sentence refers to someone with *discriminating* tastes - particularly with regards to food. A *tyro* is a novice - not someone we would expect to have very developed tastes. Eliminate it. *Wag* and *virago* do not relate to the rest of the sentence; the former means *a person given to droll humor* and the latter is *a loud and overbearing woman*. Neither of these has anything to do with food or taste, so they are most likely not the correct answers. A *libertine* - or *dissolute man* - might enjoy food, but would probably not be particularly discriminating. This leaves you with *connoisseur* and *epicure*; the former is a *discerning judge* of the arts or food, and the latter is a *person with refined tastes, especially in food or wine*.

100.   *specious* and *fallacious*

The speaker spoke well and was charming, but the audience was still dissatisfied; perhaps his claims were simply false. *Fervid* claims are characterized by intense feeling or passion; this is no way incompatible with *dazzling rhetoric and considerable charisma*, and there is no reason to believe the audience would find it off-putting. Eliminate this choice. *Picaresque* simply does not make sense in this context; it describes a specific kind of episodic narrative, often featuring a roguish hero. *Officious* means *aggressive in offering one's services* and is out of place in this sentence; *claims* are generally not officious, because they are simply statements, not offers of help. *Feckless* means *ineffective* or *lazy* - not the best choice anyway, given that it more usually describes a person, but the fact that there are no near-synonyms among the other answer choices should lead you to eliminate it. You are left with *specious* and *fallacious*, which mean, respectively, *apparently good but lacking real merit* and *logically unsound*.

101.   *tawdry* and *raffish*

The word *even* should tell you that we are looking for a word that goes beyond *excessive*, and the *countless sequins and tassels* sound a bit flashy; we want an adjective that captures these qualities. Do not be tricked into choosing *diaphanous*; while it is often used in reference to clothing or fabric, it means *sheer* or *gauzy* - not something we would associate with heavy ornamentation. *Piquant* means *pleasantly biting or interesting* and does not convey any sense of excess - eliminate it. *Aberrant* (*departing from the norm*) does not work particularly well either; although dance costumes may differ from everyday clothing, they are hardly unheard of. *Voluble* means *talkative* and is not a word used to describe clothing. *Tawdry* and *raffish* are the correct answers; they mean *gaudy* and *flashy or vulgar*, respectively.

102.   *glut* and gorge

This sentence implies that animals that hibernate do so in order to avoid having to look for food in the winter; they have to get energy from somewhere, though, so they probably eat more than usual before hibernating, and the word we choose should reflect this. *To incense* means *to anger*; using it reflexively does not make very much sense, and in any case, it would not help an animal store up energy. *To preen* means *to dress oneself smartly* or *to trim or dress fur or feathers*, and again, does not really work; if anything, preening would seem to require energy. You might think that *enervate* has something to do with gathering energy, but it actually means *to deprive of force or weaken* - eliminate it. *To recast* means *to remodel* or *to refashion*; it does not make very much sense in this sentence, unless you take it extremely figuratively and imagine the animal restructuring itself into a creature with a lower metabolism. *Glut* and *gorge* are much better choices, because both mean something like *to feed or fill to excess*.

103.   *middling* and *equivocal*

The explanation following the semi-colon, as well as the word *only*, should tell you that the efforts have been at best partially successful. *Halcyon* means *calm* or *peaceful* and therefore is irrelevant to this sentence. *Garrulous* means excessively *talkative* and again, does not make sense here. *Ecumenical* refers to something that pertains to the entire Christian religion; it would be strange if these efforts were successful only in Christian circles. Eliminate it. *Sophomoric* means *immature,* which is more commonly used to describe people or actions than facts (i.e. the results of the *efforts* here mentioned). You are left with *middling* (*mediocre* or *average*) and *equivocal* (*questionable* or *dubious*).

104.   *irascible* and *splenetic*

Someone who lashes out probably has a quick temper, so we are looking for a word that means *easily angered*. You might associate the word *recondite* with teaching or academics (it means *esoteric* or *dealing with very profound or difficult subject matter*) but it does not make sense here, where the teacher's profession is essentially unrelated to the topic of the sentence, which is her personality. *Fatuous* has an appropriately negative connotation - it means *foolish* - but there is nothing in the sentence that suggests that the teacher is dim-witted. *Stygian* means *gloomy* or *hellish*, and *turbid* means *clouded* or *confused*. They do not work particularly well as descriptions of people, so you should eliminate them. The correct answers are *irascible* and *splenetic*, which both describe someone who is easily provoked.

105.   *aptitude* and *propensity*

It is clear from the context that we are looking for a word that means something like *skills*; a word implying innate aptitude would be even better, given that the ability in question is inherited. Do not be led astray by eloquence; it does indeed imply skill, but it means *the art of using language with fluency and aptness* and does not pertain to math. *Mendacity* has a negative connotation and does not work with the rest of the sentence anyway (it means *the quality of being untruthful*). You can eliminate *recidivism* for similar reasons; it means *repeated relapse* and is often used in the context of criminal activity. *Dereliction* means *neglect* and can also be ruled out. This leaves you with *aptitude* and *propensity*, both of which describe a natural skill in or inclination towards something.

106.   *disparate* and *myriad*

This sentence focuses on the similarities between different cultures, but implies that there are many differences (only *certain* beliefs are shared). For this reason, you might guess (correctly) that the missing word means something like *different* or *varied*. If this does not occur to you while reading the sentence, though, don't worry; you should be able to rule out the incorrect choices based on how well they work in the sentence. *Inimitable* means *matchless* or *incapable of being copied*, which does not make very much sense in this context; surely no culture is perfect, and in any case, the sentence refers to all cultures regardless of whether or not the author deems them *matchless*. *Profligate* makes even less sense; it means *immoral* or *extravagant*. Again, there is no reason to believe that the author is speaking of only one kind of culture, so you can eliminate this choice as well. Palatial (*resembling a palace*) and *prolix* (*wordy* or *lengthy*) do not describe any form of culture particularly well. You are left with *disparate* and *myriad*, which work well in the sentence; the former means *dissimilar* or *distinct,* and the latter means *many* or *of a great number.*

107. *fettered* and *constrained*

The implication here is that writers and directors cannot exercise their creativity when they are forced to think about how well their movies will be received; the missing word must mean something like *burdened* or *inhibited. Obviated* makes no sense in this context; it means *to anticipate and prevent* and is generally used in the context of an event or set of circumstances. *Emaciated* means *very thin* or *wasted.* It has a negative connotation, but is probably not the best choice, unless you imagine the writers and directors being preyed upon by their concerns. In any case, it has no near synonym among the other answers, so you should be able to eliminate it. *To macerate* has a very specific meaning that clearly does apply to this sentence; it means *to soften or separate by steeping in a liquid. To satiate* means *to satisfy fully or in excess* and once again does not work in this sentence, which implies that the writers and directors are not satisfied. The correct answers are *fettered* and *constrained,* which both mean *restrained.*

108. *disinclined* and *loath*

For the most part, people attend universities so that they can find better jobs - usually jobs that don't require manual labor. Therefore, the missing word must mean something like *unwilling. Urbane* means *sophisticated* and obviously has nothing to do with factory jobs, so you can eliminate it. The only reason people might be *frantic* to accept low-paying jobs is a shortage of jobs generally, which is not the issue in question here. *Crass* and *nonplused* do not make much sense either; the former means *without refinement* or *obtuse,* and the latter means *at a loss* or *puzzled.* The best answers are *loath* (*averse* or *unwilling*) and *disinclined* (*lacking desire* or *unwilling*).

109. *retards* and *impedes*

This question requires a bit of logical thinking; if the battery is working harder but not producing more power, the cold must somehow inhibit its ability to work. *To ameliorate* clearly will not work; it means *to make better* and is the opposite of what we are looking for here. *To bedizen* (*to dress or adorn in a showy way*) simply makes no sense. *To vituperate* and *to pique* are also out of place; the former means *to berate* and the latter means *to excite* or *to wound* (*someone's feelings*). They are more commonly used in the context of social interactions, and do not work well in describing the speed of a chemical reaction. You are left with *retard* and *impede,* which both mean *to slow* or *to hinder.*

110. *degeneracy and turpitude*

Clearly, a mass murderer is not exactly a moral person. The answer probably reflects Caligula's lack of morals. *Desuetude* refers to a state of disuse; it is not the best description of someone's character. *Finesse* (*subtle skill*) and *probity* (*uprightness*) will certainly not work in this sentence. If anything, Caligula's actions reveal a complete lack of uprightness. Nor are they subtle enough to justify the use of *finesse;* a person with finesse might bend moral rules, but not so obviously ignore them. It is difficult to see what *insularity* (*pertaining to islands* or *isolated*) could have to do with the rest of the sentence; there is, for example, no indication that Caligula is following some narrow-minded moral code of his own. The best answers are *degeneracy* and *turpitude,* which mean *a state of deterioration or degradation (particularly in terms of morality)* and *depravity,* respectively.

111. *ebullient* and *blithe*

The correct answers must have something to do with *enthusiasm* and/or the ability to lift other people's spirits - *cheerful* or *optimistic,* perhaps. *Lachrymose* means *tearful* or *tending to cause tears* - the opposite of what we are looking for. *Verdant* has generally positive connotations, but it means *fresh and green* or *inexperienced* and is not the best fit in this sentence. *Edacious* means *consuming* or *voracious* and does not make sense in this context either. *Ineffable* (*incapable of being expressed*) does not work well, only because the speaker is able to describe this person's disposition (*enthusiastic*). This leaves you with *ebullient* (*overflowing with fervor or enthusiasm*) and *blithe* (*joyous* or *carefree*).

112. *felicitous* and *expedient*

This sentence deals with the scientific inaccuracy of a word, so the answer most likely means something like *accurate*. *Insouciant* means *carefree* and does not really make sense in this context - indeed, the sentence implies that scientific language is exceedingly careful. *Sententious* means *given to moralizing* or *given to pithy sayings* - neither of which are usually associated with science. *Quixotic* means *romantic* or *impulsive* (think *Don Quixote*) and once again doesn't work in the context of scientific language. *Admonitory* means *cautionary*; it is not out of the question that scientists might admonish us about certain issues, but this is hardly the point of scientific language, and you should eliminate it. You are left with *felicitous* and *expedient*, which mean, respectively, *well-suited* or *apt* and *fit for a particular purpose.*

113. *vituperation* and *obloquy*

The answer will complement *ill-will*, so we should look for a word with a fairly negative meaning that makes sense in the context of a divorce. *Doggerel*, a kind of lowbrow poetry, will certainly not work, given that it has no bearing on the subject of the sentence. *Indolence* (*idleness*) does not seem particularly likely either; it is difficult to be lazy while actively angry at someone. *Abeyance* is a temporary state of inactivity or a deferral and is similarly unsuitable in this context. *Vacillation* - or *a state of indecision* - does not fit in with ill-will either, as it would seem to imply some second thoughts or misgivings about the proceedings. This leaves you with *vituperation* and *obloquy*, which both refer to abusive and condemnatory language.

114. *disconcerting* and *ominous*

Not knowing whether a volcano is active sounds potentially dangerous and therefore worrisome, and the missing word presumably reflects this. *Inimitable* means *matchless* and has generally positive connotations - clearly not what we are looking for here. *To extenuate* means *to serve to make something seem less serious* (as in an *extenuating factor* in a court case); it does not make sense in this sentence because there is no mention of anything that requires excusing. *Trenchant* and *luculent* are also bad choices; the former means *incisive* or *effective* and the latter means *clear* or *con6vincing*. *Disconcerting* (*disturbing*) and ominous (*threatening* or *foreboding*) are the correct answers.

115. *denigrate* and *disparage*

Half of America's GDP is clearly a significant amount, so the answer probably means something like *overlook* or *discount*. *Lionize* is the near-opposite of what we are looking for; it means *to treat as a celebrity*. *Glean* does not make sense either; it means *to learn* or *to discover*, and if small businesses truly are important, surely we should want people to learn about it. *Broach* (*to mention for the first time*) will not work; it is usually followed by *the subject* or *the issue*, and in any case, the author of this sentence presumably wants this topic to be brought up and discussed. *To sanction* means *to authorize* or *to ratify* - a far cry from *discounting*. The best answers are *denigrate* (*to treat something as lacking in value*) and *disparage* (*to speak slightingly of something*).

116. *sumptuous* and *ostentatious*

As you can no doubt see from the description, Faberge eggs are highly ornamented and perhaps even a bit over-the-top; the correct answers will reflect this. *Ubiquitous* (*present everywhere*) definitely does not work; Faberge eggs are meant to stand out and be unique, and it is not as if we see replicas of them wherever we go. *Lugubrious*, which means *excessively sorrowful or melancholy*, is simply not warranted;

the author never indicates that the eggs' patterns are sorrowful in any way. Someone or something that is *prudish* is *excessively proper or modest*, which clearly is not the case of expensive luxuries like these eggs. *Incipient* means *beginning to exist*. The phrase *incredibly incipient designs* is awkward and confusing; does it imply that the designs are in some way unfinished? If you have to struggle to make a word work in the sentence, it is almost certainly not the correct answer - eliminate *incipient*. This leaves you with *sumptuous* and *ostentatious,* which mean *entailing great expense* or *lavish* and *intended to attract notice or impress*, respectively.

117.   *volatile* and *frenetic*

We are looking for a word that describes quick and random movement. *Turgid* makes little sense; it means *swollen* or *overblown.* It is not a particularly apt word for describing movement, and even if it were, *swollen* movement does not sound as if it would be fast. *Belligerent* does not work either; unless the author is speaking metaphorically, gas molecules - or molecules of any kind - cannot be *warlike* or *aggressively hostile. Irrevocable* means *unalterable* and malleable means *adaptable* - eliminate them. Clearly the particles' movements are not unalterable if they are constantly changing, and nowhere does the author imply that their movements can be influenced by humans. The correct answers are *volatile* (*unstable* or *fluctuating*) and *frenetic* (*frenzied,* here used somewhat figuratively).

118.   *inscrutable* and *enigmatic*

As the list of traits should make clear, we are looking for a word that goes beyond *bizarre and fascinating.* Given this, *prosaic* - or *commonplace* - is out of the question. You might be *incredulous* (*skeptical* or *disinclined to believe*) while reading about the octopus, but it is not a good description of the octopus itself - eliminate it. *Extant* means *in existence* and does not work well in this sentence; it is in any case difficult to be *more* in existence than something else, and this alone should dissuade you from picking this as your answer. You can also reject *nascent* (*beginning to exist*); nowhere does the sentence say that the octopus is a brand-new species. The best answers are *inscrutable* (*not easily understood*) and enigmatic (*mysterious*).

119.   *evocative and doleful*

The missing word here describes the name *The Trail of Tears,* rather than the event itself, so while the answer could be something like *sad,* it could also mean something like *descriptive. Petrous* (*stony*) will not work regardless. *Imperious* and *pugnacious* do not make sense either; the former means *overbearing,* and the latter means *quarrelsome.* It is generally best to avoid loaded or judgmental terms unless the issue in question is a clear-cut case of right and wrong; in this sentence, it is inaccurate and even insensitive to characterize the name as *overbearing. Salubrious* (*promoting health*) is also out of the question; it is hard to imagine what this would mean when describing a name or a word. This leaves you with *evocative,* meaning *suggestive* (*tending to evoke*), and *doleful,* meaning *sorrowful.*

120.   *prodigious* and *preternatural*

As this sentence makes clear, Mozart was extremely - and anomalously - skilled; the missing word should reflect that. You might think *grandiloquent* may perhaps sound promising, but it actually means *lofty* or *pretentious. Pretentious* is not a word usually used to describe a skill - you simply have the skill or you don't. In any case, its negative connotations are not justified by the sentence. *Brazen* is also a negative word; it means *shameless* or *impudent.* Again, while you might display your skills in a brazen manner, it does not make sense to describe the skills themselves as *brazen. Refractory* (*stubborn* or *disobedient*) simply does not make sense; how can an ability be *stubborn*? *Epicurean* means *fond of or adapted to luxury* and generally refers to tastes rather than skills. The best answers are *prodigious* (*extraordinary* or *wonderful*) and *preternatural* (*exceptional* with a hint of *uncanny*).

Manufactured by Amazon.ca
Bolton, ON